Working with Type
EXHIBITIONS

The photographs found on the cover and throughout this book are by David Steadman. About his work he says: "Empty space is pregnant space. The following series of images are studies of illusory empty spaces that function as metaphors for the fundamentals of exhibition design. The hand-built model environments reflect the beauty and artifice of the designed exhibition space. Nuances of light illuminate and enchant, while also high-lighting the potential activity within the construct."

A RotoVision Book
Published and distributed by RotoVision SA
Rue du Bugnon 7
CH-1299 Crans-Près-Céligny
Switzerland

RotoVision SA, Sales & Production Office
Sheridan House, 112/116A Western Road
Hove, East Sussex BN3 1DD, UK

Tel	+44 (0)1273 72 72 68
Fax	+44 (0)1273 72 72 69
E-mail	sales@rotovision.com
Website	www.rotovision.com

Distributed to the trade in the United States by:
Watson-Guptill Publications
1515 Broadway
New York, New York 10036

©2000 RotoVision SA

10 9 8 7 6 5 4 3 2 1

ISBN 2-88046-437-4

Book design by Rob Carter, John DeMao, and Sandy Wheeler

Production and separations in Singapore by ProVision Pte. Ltd.

Tel	+65 334 7720
Fax	+65 334 7721

ALTOONA RAILROADERS MEMORIAL MUSEUM
AMERICAN AIRLINES C.R. SMITH AVIATION MUSEUM
FOR LOVE OF DAYS GONE BY
GRASSLANDS
HANCOCK PARK
HOLLANDSCHE SCHOUWBURG
KELLOGG'S CEREAL CITY USA
LIBERTY SCIENCE CENTER
LOOK HEAR, ART AND SCIENCE OF THE EAR
ODYSSEY

Working with Type
EXHIBITIONS

Rob Carter

John DeMao

Sandy Wheeler

with

Barbara Fahs Charles

J. Tevere MacFadyen

Janice Majewski

Mary McLaughlin

RotoVision

CONTENTS

FOREWORD
TYPOGRAPHY AS TRANSMITTER / BARBARA FAHS CHARLES

The basic building blocks of an exhibition are five – artifacts, words (concepts and interpretation), physical design, graphic design, and lighting. Many exhibitions, of course, have additional, often very significant components – audio, video, mechanical and computer interactives, live actors, etc. – but these primary five form the core palate of every exhibition. Of these, graphic design – often primarily typography – is the connecting tissue, the carrier, the transmitter. Through typography the words have a physical presence and through the words the concepts of the exhibition and the interpretation of the artifacts are expressed most basically.

Text and typography are Siamese twins – the existence of each dependent on the other. At their zenith they are intertwined creative expressions that capture the imagination. At their nadir, they are unintelligible, illegible wasted efforts that quickly destroy all visitor interest. Words are too often the silent partners in an exhibition. As designers, we typically discuss the objects, the setting, the "mood" and the special elements of the exhibition. The quality of the texts – our basic way of understanding the goals of the exhibition – are paramount, but rarely offered the high regard they rightfully deserve. Visitors come to an exhibition, often like foreigners in a new land, not knowing what to expect. They have to learn the signs and symbols of the natives (i.e. the museum personnel, a worthy anthropological study in itself). Words, conveyed through typography, are their tools and maps for understanding. The typography and the texts must be welcoming and illuminating, at the beginning and throughout the exhibition.

Typography as the transmitter must respect the meaning of the texts. Its fundamental responsibility is to convey content. Typography also adds hierarchical clarity to the texts, signaling importance, voice, relationships, and meaning. It should entice and encourage, drawing the reader in, making museum visitors want to spend the time and energy to understand what is being presented.

At the same time, typography has other roles, both intellectual and aesthetic. Typography signals a time, a place, a culture, a style, enhancing the theme of the exhibition with subtlety or "hit-them-on-the-head" directness. It can provide unity to disparate elements or express a diversity of viewpoints. Typography at its best is a leitmotif for an exhibition, setting a tone, adding visual meaning with wit, humor, solemnity, and elegance.

Typography can also add texture and significant color. Before the computer revolution, type, in its original form as an inked element – most often metal, sometimes wood – pressed into paper, had an expressiveness that could be exploited for exhibitions. The quality and textures of the paper and the pure color of the ink added a richness no longer easily available. Now, as digitized output is increasingly being used in exhibitions, we are both gaining and losing. The sophisticated integration of typography and imagery that computers make possible is positive; the uniformity of the final product disheartening. On the other hand, sophisticated computer-driven cutters have brought dimensional type – raised, etched, or cut from almost any material – within the range of often limited museum budgets.

A theatrical comparison is not inappropriate. No matter how wonderful the script, if the actors are inaudible, it they fail to capture our attention and draw us in, we will never comprehend the full message. In the theatre of exhibition, typography, of course, doesn't act alone. The objects have the starring and primary supporting roles. Typography might be best compared to the chorus. In a Greek tragedy or the ballet, the best choruses perform with clarity and synchronized precision. Good typography requires the same attention to connection and separation, to emphasis and underscoring, to line and alignment, to rhythm and form.

Designing an
a vast underta
with a story on
a lesson o
demonstrate,
objects or arti
display. Exhi
involves the pro
appropriate form

exhibition is
king. It begins
wishes to tell,
e   hopes   to
a collection of
acts one must
bition   design
cess of finding
and authentic

expression fo

It requires the conscious arrangement of many parts, both stationary and moving, necessary in creating meaningful experiences for visitors in physical spaces. Ultimately, an exhibition is a living, three-dimensional composition to be experienced and absorbed.

Working With Type: Exhibitions is a focused investigation of typography found in the exhibition setting. Our aim is three-fold: to create greater awareness and appreciation of typography in the exhibition context, to elevate the reader's understanding of typography's critical role in the exhibition experience, and to encourage greater attention to typography in the design process.

When we began working on this book, we had to ask ourselves three key questions. The first, of course is fundamental: What is exhibition design? Exhibition design is a complex and demanding activity of making content accessible through means of interpretation and translation. The intent of the exhibition experience, from its outset, may be to inform, to educate or to entertain. Some exhibitions are meant to encourage contemplation and reflection. Exhibition design is often referred to as a three-legged stool consisting of verbal, visual, and three-dimensional disciplines. However, the process of bringing any project to fruition requires the collaboration of many individuals from diverse backgrounds and distinct areas of expertise. Typically, this process requires a delicate balancing of competing interests, ideas, and opinions held by participants. These include the institution, curators, educators, architects, content developers, graphic designers, and exhibit designers.

any content.

The second question we addressed was how broad is the territory of exhibition design? All exhibitions, regardless of topic, share the inherent dialectic between the intentions of the presenter and the experiences of the viewer. Who is displaying what and for whom? Exhibitions provide the bones for learning, exploring, and interacting. They take visitors on journeys near and far – making the inaccessible, accessible and the commonplace, extraordinary. Exhibits encompass broad categories of history, natural history, science, technology, and zoology.

Many aspects of exhibition type are shared by type found in print and other media. These similarities are manifested in the layout and visual organization of information. Many fundamental typographic principles are universal. These include form and counterform, letter, word, and line spacing, alignment, as well as contrast, rhythm, and proportion. In this book however, we have chosen to focus upon the distinctiveness of exhibition typography as it has very specific concerns and constraints that must be addressed. Some of these considerations include viewing distance, accessibility, perspective and lighting.

Working With Type: Exhibitions addresses the topics of history, typographic fundamentals, and the application of those fundamentals to exhibition design. In addition, the book contains essays written by four select individuals immersed in various aspects of exhibition design. They include two exhibition design firm principals who are also researchers, writers, and exhibit developers; a Professor who teaches exhibition design and typography; and the Accessibility Coordinator for the Smithsonian Institution. Although we present many disparate perspectives about exhibit typography, the thoughts and ideas expressed in one section of the book often resonate in others.

The book is organized into five chapters, each concentrating on a specific aspect of exhibition typography. The book opens with a foreword titled "Typography As Transmitter," by Barbara Fahs Charles, principal of Staples and Charles Ltd in Alexandria, Virginia. Chapter 1 provides an historical survey of the innovative design of three exhibitions: *Pressa*, designed by El Lissitzky in 1928; the *Building Workers' Unions Exhibition*, designed by Herbert Bayer, Walter Gropius, and László Moholy-Nagy in 1935; and *Mathematica: A World of Numbers... and Beyond*, designed by the office of Charles and Ray Eames in 1961. Chapter 2 focuses on typographic considerations specific to the field of exhibition design. Here, we discuss the formal language of typography through the topics of Legibility, Selecting Typefaces, Structure, and Special Considerations. Chapter 3, "Readable Labels: The Perceived Conflict Between Form and Function," is written by Janice Majewski, the Accessibility Coordinator for the Smithsonian Institution. Chapter 4, "Projects," presents an inventory of nineteen exemplary exhibitions. Chapter 5, "A Closer Look," observes and discusses these projects in greater detail. Each of the exhibits has been completed within the past decade.

Of note, are two insightful essays running along the outside edges of the book. The first, "Education of an Exhibit Designer," by Mary McLaughlin of Virginia Commonwealth University begins at Chapter 1. The second, "Windows, Maps, and Labels: Rethinking the Role of Typography in Exhibition Design," is by J. Tevere MacFadyen, principal of Main Street Design, Inc. in Cambridge. This essay begins at Chapter 4. We encourage you to turn the book lengthwise to read and contemplate these essays.

HISTORICAL
SURVEY

EDUCATION OF AN EXHIBIT DESIGNER
ESSAY BY MARY MCLAUGHLIN
MOST EXHIBIT DESIGN PROJECTS START OUT AS A ROUGH OUTLINE OF CONTENT, SOME IDENTIFIABLE MAJOR POINTS TO BE MADE, A STACK OF IMAGE IDEAS AND

During the 20th century, exhibition design evolved as a fascinating attempt to unite design practice and theory. Some of the earliest efforts to explore communication within the context of three-dimensional space occurred in the Soviet Union and in Germany at the Bauhaus. Here, projects and experiments contributed to a new language of vision, a language fueled by the spirit of a new age, a response to new technology and materials, and by the inventive use of words and images. From these beginnings, the relationship of typography to exhibition design has evolved steadily, responding continually to social, scientific, and technological changes, and most notably to the impact and influence of electronic media. This chapter surveys three exemplary exhibitions, providing an historical context for understanding the use of typography in contemporary exhibition design.

PHOTOGRAPHS, SOME TEXT AS YET UNOPERATED ON, AND AN EMPTY SPACE. ¶ TO ME, THE WHOLE IDEA OF AN EXHIBIT DESIGN IS TO TAKE THAT EMPTY SPACE, AND LET IT

Leninswerke in 50 Sprachen

SOVIET PAVILION AT THE INTERNATIONAL PRESS EXHIBITION, PRESSA, COLOGNE 1928 EL LISSITZKY

El (Lazar Markovich) Lissitzky (1890 – 1941), is perhaps most well known as the individual who embodied the Russian constructivist movement of the 1920s. Through his tireless and enthusiastic work as a typographer, painter, architect, graphic designer, and photographer, he was able to promote the most progressive artistic tendencies and political ideals of his time. Unlike many of his contemporaries and those of later generations, Lissitzky saw art and modern technology as one. He was able to integrate the two with great imagination and wit while keeping his feet firmly planted in every aspect of reality.

Any current study of typography and exhibition design benefits greatly from close examination of his work. The student of Lissitzky learns volumes about construction and detail, asymmetry in composition, abstract geometric form and its relationship to typographic form. Students learn about space – psychological space, spaces for living and learning, and they learn about passion.

During 1927 – 1929, Lissitzky immersed himself almost entirely in typographic projects along with the design and installation of trade exhibitions. Working with physical space allowed him to extend his love of typography onto an environmental scale. In many ways, this was a natural progression from his earlier *Proun Space* and the Dresden and Hanover "Demonstration Rooms" where he sought new methods of displaying art. He states his intentions as "installing works in a setting that forced the viewer to respond to and initiate changes in the environment, in an attempt to achieve some of the same education of consciousness that the art itself promoted."

In 1927, Lissitzky designed the exhibition, catalogue, poster, and invitation card for the *All-Union Printing Trades Exhibition*, in Moscow. This favorable experience led to his commission the following year to manage the design and production of the Soviet Pavilion at the International Press Exhibition, *Pressa*, in Cologne.

1
Designs for a flag stand that was never built. Lissitzky wrote of these designs, "...They're all crazy and think we're rolling in money. I received a tender for the outside structure – 49,500 marks... I'll practically have to make fresh designs. Have to negotiate and make transactions. Art, where art thou?... I'm now afraid that I'll lose the general view of the whole thing."

2
Preliminary sketch of the entrance hall. Lissitzky had originally planned for nine moving belts, but due to budget constraints had to settle on six.

BECOME THE THEATRE IN WHICH THE CONTENT, THE IMAGES, THE DEMONSTRATIONS, ETC., ACT OUT THE DRAMA OF THEIR RELATIONSHIPS IN A MEANINGFUL WAY.

I ENCOURAGE STUDENTS TO THINK OF THE EMPTY SPACE AS A THEATRE, SO THEY WILL BEGIN TO THINK OF THE EXHIBIT'S COMPONENT PARTS AS HAVING A LIVING ROLE IN

THE VISITOR'S PROCESS OF UNDERSTANDING THE EXHIBIT CONTENT. THE RELATIONSHIPS MODEL IS KEY FOR ME, SINCE CONCEPTUALLY IT FORCES THE DESIGNER TO FOCUS

3

Upon entering *Pressa*, visitors were met by two structural elements, the Transmission Belts and the Red Star. Lissitzky used oversized conveyor belts to present examples of Soviet Press. These six "moving walls" were symbolic of both the web printing process and the six republics of Russia. The large Red Star was, according to Lissitzky, intended to represent the Soviet constitution by a complex system of symbolic relationships. (See preceding spread)

4, 5

"The Press of the Red Army" and "The Press and the Soviet Woman" are two examples of thematic zones within *Pressa*. The form and construction of these figures, as well as their typographic treatment, reflect the content they present.

6

One visitor to the *Pressa* exhibition observed, "It shows the growth of cultural interests and the increasing hunger for intellectual improvement; above all, however, it shows the control which is exercised by the newspapers over industries, educational establishments, and organizations."

20

The objective of the Russian Pavilion in Cologne, was to demonstrate advances in the press sector of the socialist state and to increase international understanding between the West and other nations concerning issues of philosophy, politics, and religion. The content of the exhibition was organized within twenty "demonstration rooms" in addition to thematic zones that carried contemporary issues such as industrialization and electrification; the living conditions of the working class; trades unions; agriculture; and social life within the young Soviet State.

Pressa was accomplished by the collaborative efforts of some thirty-seven artists, designers, photographers, film-makers and engineers, from both Germany and the Soviet Union. For the first time, photography and photomontage techniques were employed successfully in an exhibit environment to enhance both the political-propagandistic nature of the content and the overall multimedia experience.

Pressa remains one of the finest examples of a creative collective in exhibition design. It established a precedence for many of the contemporary issues that museum developers and designers wrestle with today, including the variance of ideas, cultures, and values in our society and the ever-present need to diversify expertise and the pool of participants.

4

5

6

BUILDING WORKERS' UNIONS EXHIBITION BERLIN, 1935
HERBERT BAYER, WALTER GROPIUS, LÁSZLÓ MOHOLY-NAGY

1

Many advances in the field of exhibition design were launched during the early part of the twentieth century by artists and designers who formed creative liaisons to explore and experiment with new concepts, methods, and materials.

New visions in the area of exhibition design were developed by members of the Bauhaus, or by individuals once affiliated with the institution. A key player in this development was Herbert Bayer whose experimental spirit brought new insight to the practice of typography, advertising design, and exhibition design. Adhering to the overriding philosophy of the Dessau Bauhaus, Bayer was committed to integrating all aspects of functional design, including exhibition design, into the greater sphere of architecture.

Bayer was impressed with and influenced by the constructivist work of El Lissitzky, as well as by the technological and scientific ideas of László Moholy-Nagy. At the Bauhaus, he established a Workshop for Typography and Advertising in which he and his students could

experiment freely with new forms and techniques. Bayer's design for the "Universal" typeface is representative of his experimental nature and desire to express concepts with clarity, explicitness, and precision. These attitudes flooded naturally into the realm of exhibition design as well, where verbal, visual, and structural elements were integrated into a greater system.

In 1935, seven years after resigning from the Bauhaus, Bayer collaborated with Walter Gropius, Marcel Breuer, and László Moholy-Nagy in the design of an exhibition for the *Baugewerkschafts Ausstellung (Building Workers' Unions Exhibition)* in Berlin. Five years earlier, in 1930, while working on a section of the exhibition *The Room of Our Time,* Bayer created a sketch called *Diagram of Field of Vision.* This diagram became the philosophical foundation of Bayer's approach to exhibition design and was updated for the *Building Workers' Unions Exhibition.* The diagram illustrates the ability of a human figure to view visual panels set at varying angles from a central position in a hypothetical

1
The functional elements of point, line, and plane provided the visual and structural basis of the exhibition, and the honest, down-to-earth, gutsy attitude associated with working and workers.

THE AGENT FOR CONTINUITY THROUGHOUT THE EXHIBITION. 1 IN ANY EXHIBIT THERE ARE MANY DIFFERENT KINDS OF WORD VOICES, ALL OF WHICH NEED TO BE HEARD.

24

2

With the exception of a stencilled modern typeface with extreme contrast between thick and thin strokes, and linear hairline serifs, the exhibit made use of a collection of sanserif types. One of these was a typeface reminiscent of the "Universal" typeface designed by Herbert Bayer. (See preceding spread)

3

Typography was applied with variety to a wide range of structural components, including rhythmic fence-like structures with text running horizontally along slats, black sanserif type set justified on white panels, and white type set flush-left, ragged right on black panels.

4

Bayer's *Diagram of 360 Degrees Field of Vision*, 1935, represented a revolutionary way of thinking about how viewers see and perceive exhibition space.

5

Bayer's Universal typeface was an experiment to reduce the alphabet to a single set of geometric forms, and to maximize their differences for optimal legibility. Consisting of a few curves, three different angles, and vertical and horizontal lines, the typeface epitomizes Bayer's commitment to rational and functional form. Shown here are the regular and condensed variations.

exhibition space. The substance of the field-of-vision idea is to reveal the fact that an exhibition is a visual environment wherein the viewer takes an active role in the viewing experience. Bayer perceived an exhibition installation as an environment where objects are not hung statically along a wall, but where typography, images, and artifacts are dynamically and rhythmically integrated as a structural system.

For the *Building Workers' Unions Exhibition*, Bayer designed a space that provided the visitor with an opportunity to become part of the viewing experience, to engage in an active and honest dialogue with the elements of the exhibition rather than to assume the role of a passive spectator. Mechanized louvers shifted automatically to reveal different images, while footprints placed strategically on the floor guided the visitor through the space.

The exhibition consisted of modular architectonic structures serving as a foundation and backdrop for a profusion of text and images. At a moment when the eye finds an opportunity to rest, it is again swept onto a new visual path. Moments of repose exist for the viewer, but the installation's asymmetrical charisma demands attentiveness. It is an excitable, free-flowing space characterized by dynamic scale shifts, use of varied materials and textures, and typography ranging from the emphatic to the subtle.

When it came to typography, Bayer remained an adamant functionalist. Typographical treatments within the exhibition tempered the more active role of images and three-dimensional components. While typography was understated and carefully considered in terms of typeface selection and legibility, it was also varied in scale, use of upper- and lowercase letters, and text configuration.

Perhaps the most important thing to be learned from this historical exhibition is that typography is not simply applied as an afterthought, or as a separate running narrative, but that it is integrated visually and verbally with other exhibition components into a dynamic visual field.

3

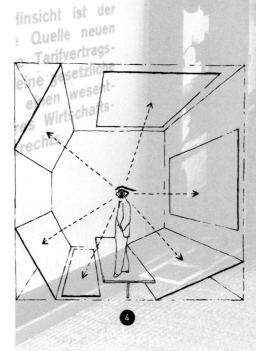

4

abcdefghijkl
mnpqrstuvw
xyzag   dd

abcdefghi
jklmnopqr
stuvwxyz
a   d d

5

MATHEMATICA: A WORLD OF NUMBERS... AND BEYOND, LOS ANGELES, 1961
EAMES OFFICE

Mathematica: A World of Numbers... and Beyond, was designed by the Eames Office for the IBM corporation. The exhibit opened in 1961, at the California Museum of Science and Industry in Los Angeles, and has become the exhibit against which all later exhibit work focusing on science is measured. Although the strength of this exhibit lies in the amazing power of its creative visuals and displays to describe and explain complex mathematical ideas to the layman, typography also plays a highly graphic and informational role.

A near riot of typefaces, fonts, sizes, and weights, conjoined with graphics, models, films, noise-making exhibits, and interactive displays create an engaging participatory event for the exhibit-goer. Charles and Ray Eames purposely approached their topic with the concept that all science, mathematics being no exception, is fun, and learning about it could also be enjoyable.

Graphic panels, walls, and ceiling-hung boards use a variety of typographic treatments, illustrations and photographs to explain mathematical phenomena, carry quotes, or describe topics. Two fifty-foot walls, a "History Wall" and an "Image Wall," enclose the three-dimensional exhibit components on two of their sides and describe, respectively, the chronological development of mathematics including biographies of mathematical greats and mathematical breakthroughs on one, and visual explanations and textual descriptions of mathematical principals on the other.

1
The extensive, and rare use of all caps goes beyond the exhibit name and subtitle to encompass much of the typography that is used. The relatively large scale of much of it, mitigates legibility problems that would normally arise.

©2000 Lucia Eames dba Eames Office (www.eamesoffice.com)

AND VOICES ASSIGNED TO "ACTIVE" PARTS OF THE INFORMATION. WHEN IT IS POSSIBLE TO CONCEIVE OF EACH VOICE EXPRESSED IN A DIFFERENT SIZE, WEIGHT, AND/OR

ESSENTIAL TO THE WHOLENESS OF A THING. THEY STRUGGLE WITH QUESTIONS OF INTERPRETATION, HIERARCHY, AND ORGANIZATION. THEY HAVE TO STOP BLAMING ANY

2
The rich mixture of typefaces, sizes, and settings, and their application to many visual planes throughout the three-dimensional space adds visual interest, dimension, and energy to the exhibit space. (See preceding spread)

3
The "Image Wall," which demonstrates and clarifies mathematical principles, reflects the Eames' exceptional ability to interpret and express concepts in visual form.

4
The title frames from four peep shows reveal eclectic typefaces combined with graphic elements to create distinctiveness and visual interest for visitors.

3

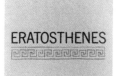

4

5

©2000 Lucia Eames dba Eames Office (www.eamesoffice.com)

6

5
Lucia Eames Demetrios and her children at the peep show machines. The range of typographic applications addressed in *Mathematica* was broad, from single expository print panels to time-dependent, kinetic film typography.

6
The "History Wall," with a magnitude and multitude of textual content that is seldom attempted in current exhibition design, is organized with clear heads and detailed descriptions underneath. The biographies are all set in caps, condensed – an unusual approach for the quantity of text.

The original exhibition was accompanied by five, two minute films, "peep shows" – four animated, one live action – explaining various mathematical principles. These were eventually removed from the exhibition due to technical problems; but they are a testament to the Eames' desire to reach the audience in every possible way.

The most striking aspect of the exhibition design was to encourage visitors to be involved as active participants in the content, thereby deepening the learning process. The Eames' hoped to increase understanding of this

content by interpreting it through the visual, aural, and tactile senses.

It is profound that the typography in *Mathematica* fulfills its expected role as a dedicated carrier of information. However, it is perhaps more significant that the designers involved with this exhibit understood the transcendent potential of typography to influence the visual and emotional impact of a three-dimensional space.

CONFUSION ON IMMALLEABLE INFORMATION, AND, AS EDWARD TUFTE WRITES, "FIND DESIGN STRATEGIES THAT REVEAL DETAIL AND COMPLEXITY." ¶ SO THE FIRST WAY WE

2

2

TYPOGRAPHIC
CONSIDERATIONS
FOR EXHIBITION DESIGN

ULTIMATE CHOICES OF TYPE SIZE, FACE, OR CONFIGURATION, IT IS PRIMARILY AN EXERCISE IN AWARDING EMPHASIS TO ASPECTS OF THE EXHIBIT STORY, AND IDENTIFYING

LEGIBILITY

Letters and words are legible when they are easily identifiable and distinguishable one from another. Letters are more or less legible depending upon a number of fundamental attributes, including weight, width, shape, size, proportion, and the dynamic relationships of form and counterform. Legibility in words is directly related to word shape and internal pattern, visual factors that provide every word with a unique visual structure. Word shape and internal pattern are controlled by three factors: the individual letterforms composing the word, the manner in which the letterforms are commingled, and the spacing between letters within words. Readability is a less easily defined and agreed upon term and is often considered an extension of legibility. Readability is concerned with the overall process of deciphering the typographic information. It is affected most significantly by the relationships of type size, line length, and interline spacing. For optimum readability, these three factors must be carefully proportioned. For example, type size affects line length, and line length affects interline spacing. Appropriate line length is essential to enable a rhythmic flow in reading. Lines that are too short require excess eye movement, thus tiring the reader; lines that are too long make it more difficult to return to the starting points of subsequent lines. Similarly, appropriate interline spacing prevents lines of type from appearing either too close or too far apart, conditions that significantly disrupt reading patterns and the interpretation of information.

EXHIBIT, IT IS THE TYPOGRAPHY THAT WILL POSITION ITSELF ACROSS A WIDE VARIETY OF SURFACES: ARCHITECTURE, EXHIBIT FURNITURE, MONITORS, INSTRUCTION PANELS,

Understanding the anatomy of letterforms is a more complex task than it may appear. It requires familiarity with the various component parts that constitute individual letterforms and their interrelationships of stroke weight and stress, heights and widths. Designers who understand the complexity of typographic forms are better able to appreciate the subtle visual relationships existing within and between letters, words, lines, and paragraphs.

1
This display of the alphabet reveals the nomenclature associated with typographic anatomy. This terminology has evolved over the centuries, and knowing it adds immeasurably to a designer's typographic vocabulary and ability to communicate about type.

2
When set into words and text, all typographic characters are aligned upon a baseline. The tops of lowercase letters run along a meanline; the height of capital letters along a capline. The interval between a baseline and the height of lowercase letters is known as the x-height.

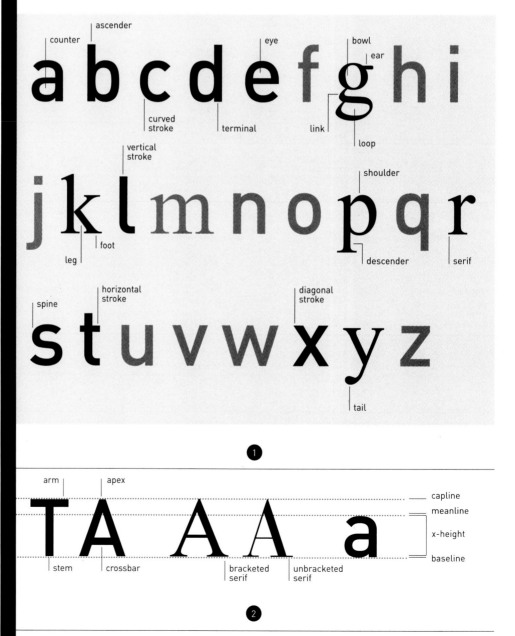

1

2

PROPORTION

The proportions of letterforms are determined by several different relationships: stroke height to weight, height to width, x-height in relation to cap height, and length of ascenders and descenders. Each of these factors is influenced by the relative contrast of the thickness and thinness of various strokes in individual letterforms.

Compliance to ADA (American with Disabilities Act) guidelines requires that "letters and numbers on signs shall have a width-to-height ratio between 3:5 and 1:1, and a stroke width-to-height ratio between 1:5 and 1:10". These guidelines offer an excellent rule of thumb, but equally important when considering the proportions of type are a trained eye and common sense.

3
The ratio of height to width determines where a letterform falls on a scale from condensed to expanded. The wider the letterform in relation to its height the more expanded it will appear. Conversely, the narrower the width compared to its height the more condensed the letterform appears. Both highly condensed and expanded typefaces impair legibility.

4
The ratio between the various stroke widths helps to establish a letterform's weight and visual signature.

5
The visual tension created by the interplay of thick and thin strokes in letters provides textural and visual variety.

6
The size of the x-height in relation to cap height, ascenders, and descenders, strongly influences the proportions and appearances of letterforms. Letterforms with large x-heights appear larger than letterforms with smaller x-heights when comparing typefaces of the same point size. All things being equal, letterforms with larger x-heights are usually more legible than those with smaller x-heights. Compare in this example the x-heights of Din Medium and Times New Roman.

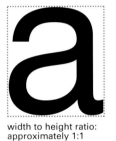

width to height ratio: approximately 1:1

width to height ratio: approximately 2:3

3

4

5

48 point Din Medium

48 point Times New Roman

6

TAILORED RELATIONSHIP WITH PARTICULAR THREE-DIMENSIONAL FEATURES: EDGES, CORNERS, RIMS. THIS IS AN EXERCISE IN CONCEPTUALIZING THE SURFACES AND THEIR

FORM AND COUNTERFORM

The balance between form (the black parts of letters, or positive spaces) and counterform (the white parts of letters, or negative spaces) are indispensable to legibility and the identification of letters and words. The synergy between these two perceived spatial zones provides type with a unique character and structure.

7
The integrity of letterforms is determined by a careful balancing act of form, normally expressed as black or a color, and the integral counterform comprising the space or spaces contained within the form. These two visual aspects are both interdependent, and inseparable.

8
Letter spacing that is too tight makes it difficult for readers to distinguish individual letterforms. As a result, letters appear to merge together, losing their identity, and therefore making it difficult to read words and phrases. Letter spacing that is too loose has the opposite effect: letters appear to float apart, disrupting the natural flow of words into lines. Optimum letter spacing for 48 point Din Medium is highlighted in this example.

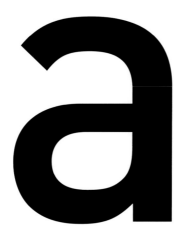

SPACING

Letter, word and line spacing is particularly important in exhibition design, as the sizes of type in exhibits is consistently larger than those used in print. A critical eye is necessary for ensuring proper word and line spacing so that a consistent texture, tone, and flow are achieved to facilitate ease of reading.

Achieving proper typographic spacing is a matter of finding the appropriate proportional relationships between letters, words, and

type
48 point Din Medium, -20 tracking

type
48 point Din Medium, -10 tracking

type
48 point Din Medium, -3 tracking

type
48 point Din Medium, -1.5 tracking

type
48 point Din Medium, 0 tracking

t y p e
48 point Din Medium, +25 tracking

t y p e
48 point Din Medium, +100 tracking

lines. By considering letter spaces within words (the smallest units of typographic space), and relating them to word spaces within lines and line spaces within paragraphs (a progressive spatial scheme), the designer is able to find just the right proportional balance.

The intrinsic visual characteristics of specific typefaces selected for use in an exhibition must also be taken into consideration when in the process of spacing typographic units.

Designers must be particularly sensitive to the irregularities and peculiarities of individual letterforms and adjust them optically for a consistent spatial appearance.

Kerning, the process of removing or adding minute increments of space between awkward character pairs is absolutely essential. This process is most critical for larger sizes of type.

9

It is common practice to sensitively adjust word spacing to the established proportions of letter spacing. Excess word spacing creates disjointed and discontinuous text. Too little word spacing makes it harder to group individual words into phrases while reading, thus severely compromising readability. The bottom example in this figure displays appropriate word spacing in relationship to letter spacing.

10

Appropriate line spacing ensures that readers are carried easily from one line to the next. It is always problematic to set lines of type too closely together. In most exhibition settings, text can be presented with more generous line spacing. Within limits, greater spacing does not significantly affect readability in exhibition text. However, it slows the reading process, appears calmer, and creates a more enunciated reading of the text. Optimum line spacings are highlighted in this example.

11

An important task is always to carefully and deliberately kern character pairs to ensure consistent optical letter spacing within words. Arrows in the top example point to kerning problems that have been resolved in the bottom example.

Exhibition

Exhibitiontypographyislikebackgroundmusic.

Exhibition

Exhibition typography is like background

Exhibition

Exhibition typography is like background music.

9

type
type

11

Exhibition typography is like background music. Most people notice it only when it is noticeably bad. When it's good, typography calls less attention to itself than to the stories it's trying to tell, the mood it hopes to create, the content it seeks to express.

Exhibition typography is like background music. Most people notice it only when it is noticeably bad. When it's good, typography calls less attention to itself than to the stories it's trying to tell, the mood it hopes to create, the content it seeks to express.

Exhibition typography is like background music. Most people notice it only when it is noticeably bad. When it's good, typography calls less attention to itself than to the stories it's trying to tell, the mood it hopes to create, the content it seeks to express.

Exhibition typography is like background music. Most people notice it only when it is noticeably bad. When it's good, typography calls less attention to itself than to the stories it's trying to tell, the mood it hopes to create, the content it seeks to express.

Exhibition typography is like background music. Most people notice it only when it is noticeably bad. When it's good, typography calls less attention to itself than to the stories it's trying to tell, the mood it hopes to create, the content it seeks to express.

10

LINE LENGTH

Determining line lengths for exhibit text is a crucial undertaking, for text is the interpretive bridge between artifact and fact, seeing and perceiving.

The process is considerably removed from the conventional concerns of publication design, in that exhibits are born from the efforts, knowledge, and expertise of a team of individuals – project directors, architects, engineers, writers, and graphic designers.

Throughout the exhibition design process, not a single aspect of an exhibit can be unilaterally considered; all members of the team work together, synthesizing the content, the form, and the structure into an intelligible and accessible whole. Therefore, decisions regarding the line lengths of text are inextricably linked to an exhibit's content and structural components.

Before making any decision regarding line length, the following basic questions should be asked. What is the nature, length, and

12
There are 66 characters in this line of text. It is considered to be of optimum length for most typefaces and for most type sizes viewed at the intended viewing distance. Remember that word spaces and punctuation are also counted as characters when determining line length.

13
Typeface, type size, letter and word spacing, and line length are all interrelated variables that should be considered when solving text problems. It is advisable to output text at actual size and to view it at a distance that closely approximates the exhibit setting. Any one of the above variables can then be changed to improve the text. Several evaluations of actual size output may be necessary before the optimum result is achieved.

Exhibition typography is like bac

n typograph

Most people r

Exhibition typography is like background music. Most people notice it only when it is noticeably bad. When it's good, typography calls less attention to itself than to the stories it's trying to tell, the mood it hopes to create, the content it seeks to express.

a

hierarchy of the content? What typefaces will be used? What are the sizes of the panels or planar surfaces of exhibit structures? At what distances will the text be read?

Line length should be measured by the number of typographic characters per line. This will then be translated into a standard unit of measurement, such as inches or centimeters. The optimum number of characters per line for exhibition text is 45 to 75. It is generally accepted that 66 characters per line is an optimum number. Line lengths falling outside of these parameters should be carefully assessed on the basis of how the foregoing questions have been answered. At the same time, it is important to remember that these guidelines are not ultimatums.

It is always sound practice to create prototypes of text at actual size to assess readability, and to make necessary adjustments.

14
In these simulated graphic panels, line lengths play a role in visual aesthetics. Panel *a* appears choppy and fragmented due to very short line lengths; panel *b* appears simple, relaxed, and very readable.

round music. Most people notice

is like backg

otice it only w

Exhibition typography is like background music. Most people notice it only when it is noticeably bad. When it's good, typography calls less attention to itself than to the stories it's trying to tell, the mood it hopes to create, the content it seeks to express.

b

CONTINUITY IN A COMPLETELY DIFFERENT WAY. ¶ UNLIKE A BOOK, THE CONTINUITY OF AN EXHIBIT MAY BE EXPRESSED AMONG LIKE ELEMENTS IN A LAYERED SCHEME THAT

15

Located in an exterior pedestrian environment, the typography on these panels is sized and positioned for ease of readability, interpretation, and hierarchical clarity. The size of the typographic elements adheres to ADA guidelines for viewing distance. (Exhibition: Hancock Park, Sussman/ Prejza & Co. Inc.)

16

The most important consideration for making decisions about the color of type and its background is value contrast. ADA guidelines recommend contrast of at least 70%. The second most important consideration is hue contrast. Dark type on light backgrounds offers the most legible combinations. Color should never be considered outside the environment in which it is viewed. Consider the color combinations in this example: *a* highly legible due only to strong value contrast; *b* very legible, but less so than black on white; *c* very legible due to strong hue and value contrasts; *d* less legible due to weak hue contrast; *e* less legible due to weak value contrast.

SCALE

The scale of typography is an important legibility concern. Conditions that should be taken into consideration when determining type sizes include the positioning of type in its environment, viewing distances, fields of vision, lighting conditions, and the color and value contrasts of type and its background. The scale of type should be adjusted in relation to these factors to make it most visible and accessible.

COLOR

The relationship between the color of type and its background is influenced by the specific hue, value, intensity, and color temperature of each color. Color considerations in exhibition design are all the more important due to the variable conditions of illumination and environment. In the controlled spaces of a building, color can be orchestrated precisely. In exterior spaces, light, shade, and changing weather conditions greatly affect color perception.

color

a

color

b

color

c

color

d

color

e

BACK-LIT TYPOGRAPHY

Back-lighting can be used to substantially increase the intensity and depth of the visual forms. Careful control of the intensity of the light source is necessary to keep the edges from flaring and interfering with the legibility of the letterforms. Typefaces with very thin strokes can also suffer from excessive flaring in those strokes, impairing their legibility. Back-lit typography in large amounts can be tiring to the eyes. External lighting must be well controlled to prevent interference.

PROJECTED TYPOGRAPHY

Projected typography must be carefully controlled to make sure that it is properly focused on the presentation surface. The greater the projection distance, the more difficult it is to read due to a loss in intensity and softening of edges. Exaggeration and distortion of letterforms by curving or rotating the projection surface adds dimension, depth and visual intrigue.

17

The use of back-lit typography in this exhibit provides a luminescence, depth, and intensity that would be impossible to achieve using more conventional application methods. (Exhibition: *World of Life*, California Science Center, West Office Exhibition Design)

18

Type can be projected onto images, objects, and other type for a visually resonant, layered effect. Care should be taken to preserve the fidelity of type when readability is required.

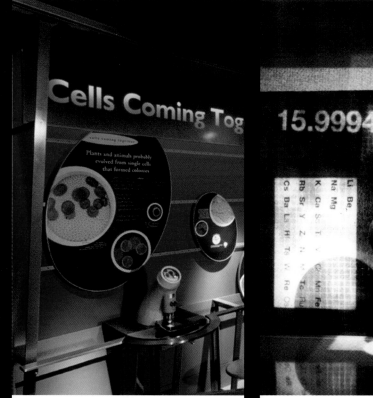

17

18

TYPOGRAPHY – SIZE, WEIGHT OR CONFIGURATION – BUT BY SIZE OR "PRESENCE" OF THE GRAPHIC SURFACE ITSELF. ¶ A WONDERFUL EXAMPLE OF THIS KIND OF LAYERED

THREE-DIMENSIONAL TYPOGRAPHY

When typography is expressed three-dimensionally, it appears architectonic in form, and is capable of redefining space and creating resonant spatial experiences for visitors. At a monumental scale, three-dimensional typography activates the space where visitors experience it both visually through changes of perspective, and physically by influencing the movements and focus of the audience.

Type is conventionally seen and perceived as flat letters on a two-dimensional plane. When it is taken out of this expected context and provided with depth, new legibility concerns arise. In the translation from two to three dimensions, the integrity of the proportions of the original typeface must be maintained. This requires very careful drawings made to scale, so that at the time of construction nothing is lost in translation.

19
The monumental typographic forms in this space serve as kiosks to help the visitor navigate the space, and gain access to important exhibit information. (Exhibition: *Taxi*, Trickett & Webb Limited)

20
A three-dimensional letter *E* functions as a display unit for Elvis memorabilia. (Exhibition: *Elvis is in the Building*, The Rock and Roll Hall of Fame and Museum, Pentagram)

19

20

Type elements translated into three dimensions are perceived as objects in space, functioning not only to contribute in the communication of an exhibit's message, but also to define and structure exhibition space. This function broadens the parameters of typographic legibility, for the type must be decoded both as a message carrier and a mediator of space. It is recommended that scale models and full-scale prototypes are made and evaluated.

21

22

21
Circular canopies suspended strategically throughout the exhibit mark different thematic zones. Condensed Gill Sans letters in all caps are pin-mounted, adding further dimensionality to the structures. (Exhibition: *World of Life*, California Science Center, West Office Exhibition Design)

22
Typographic prominence is gained when three-dimensional letters are surface mounted in three-dimensional spaces. Garamond is a typeface design that is not compromised when translated into three-dimensions. (Exhibition: *Odyssey*, The Maritime Discovery Center, West Office Exhibition Design)

TOGETHER IN FRONT OF THE SPECIMENS ARE SEVERAL SMALLER INFORMATION UNITS. THE UNITS ARE ALMOST ANTHROPOMORPHIC – EACH A POLE WITH A "HEAD" ON TOP –

TYPOGRAPHY IN SPACE AND TIME

Typography meant to be experienced temporally plays a distinct role in exhibition design. Most often it is encountered as a component of video, film, and/or interactive multimedia. While this chapter does not focus on issues of legibility within this specific realm, it is important to mention that legibility concerns are expanded when working with type in motion, for time (issues of pacing and sequencing) as well as space must be articulated.

23

Consistent typographic treatment among all elements of this exhibit, including any interactive or motion graphics, helps to establish an integrated and holistic experience for the visitor. (Rock and Roll Hall of Fame and Museum, Interactive Interface, The Burdick Group)

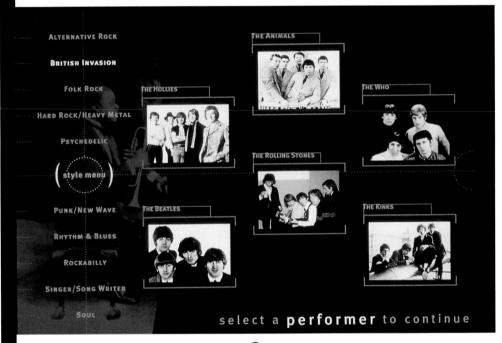

select a **performer** to continue

23

AND EACH PROVIDES A BRIEF BIT OF INFORMATION. THE VISITOR ENCOUNTERS SIMILAR CLUSTERS THROUGHOUT THE EXHIBIT. THEY ARE STATIONED LIKE A GROUP OF

VISUAL ACUITY

Acuity is a term referring to the sharpness of perception. Visual acuity refers to the precision with which one perceives visual form. In the typographic realm, visual acuity (or the lack of it), directly impacts legibility, and in turn, the readability of typography. Typographic acuity demands that viewers are able to see and interpret typographic information under normal and adverse conditions. Acuity concerns include typeface and style, letterform proportions, viewing distance, color and value contrast, lighting conditions, and general environmental concerns. Other factors affecting typographic acuity are discernment of the shapes of individual letterforms, the relative thickness of letter strokes, height-to-width ratios, size, letter spacing, and the arrangement of type in space.

24
One of the most obvious factors affecting legibility is the size of the type and the distance at which it is viewed. It is difficult to determine a formula that accommodates the viewing needs of a wide range of individuals, takes into consideration the fact that viewing conditions can be far from favorable, or acknowledges that type is often read from an angle. Nonetheless, ADA guidelines offer a reasonable plan: for each 25 feet of viewing distance, the cap height of letters should be increased in size by one inch.

25
High acuity is a matter of paying attention to details. For example, if using all capitals is a requirement, ADA guidelines recommend a wider than normal tracking (110 – 120%). But remember: in almost every situation, words set in upper- and lowercase letters are more readable than those set in all uppercase letters.

26
The upper halves of both upper- and lowercase letters feature more recognizable visual cues than the lower halves.

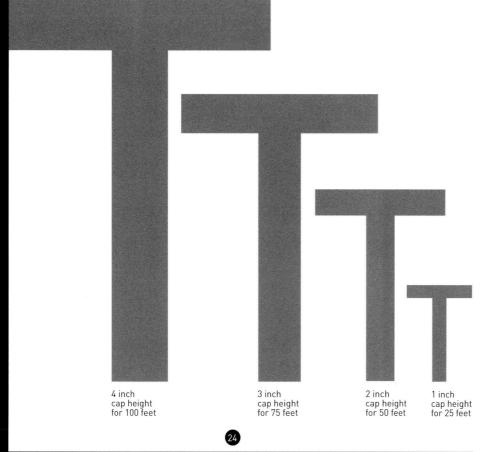

4 inch
cap height
for 100 feet

3 inch
cap height
for 75 feet

2 inch
cap height
for 50 feet

1 inch
cap height
for 25 feet

EXHIBITION
EXHIBITION
top: normal tracking
bottom: 110% tracking

46

With an explosive increase in the number of new typeface designs, the task of selecting appropriate typefaces for any task becomes increasingly important. Choosing typefaces for exhibitions, however, is further complicated by scale factors and by the fact that type is viewed in three-dimensional environments. The type selection process is never simply a matter of personal preference. It is, rather, a process requiring a thoughtful consideration of the specific needs of the audience and the nature of the exhibition's content. Exhibitions geared to general audiences will out of necessity require typefaces that are readable for both young people just learning to read and older people whose vision has severely declined; though readability is a relative concern and open to interpretation. The amount and size of text, reading distances, lighting, typographic production and manufacture, and the configuration of the exhibit space are all important considerations. Because type is viewed, it is very important to consider the nature and scope of the exhibition's content. By virtue of shape and proportion, letters possess personalities, attitudes, and emotive qualities that may seem to offer just the right conceptual fit. Typefaces can also elude to specific time periods, environments, and social and political milieus. Visual distinctions are sometimes very subtle and not easy to identify. Typefaces may "feel" right or seem to reveal just the right mood because of a very subtle characteristic such as a unique serif, a peculiar character, or a shape that beckons to another time and place.

INFORMATION AND FACILITATES UNDERSTANDING FOR THE VISITOR. THE CLUSTER SEPARATES INFORMATION BY TYPE, WHILE AT THE SAME TIME STRUCTURALLY EXPRESSING

1

Old Style:
Inspired by carved Roman capitals, Old Style letters possess medium stroke contrast and oblique, bracketed serifs.

Transitional:
Developed during the 1700s, Transitionals possess medium to high stroke contrast and sharp, bracketed, slightly slanted serifs.

Modern:
Modern typefaces, first developed in the late 1700s are characterized by medium to high stroke contrast and thin, unbracketed serifs.

Slab Serif:
Known also as Egyptian, these typefaces, first introduced in the early 1800s, possess little or no stroke contrast; their serifs are thick and square, and they possess a larger x-height than earlier styles.

Sanserif:
During the early 1800s, typefaces without serifs began to appear. Generally, these forms have squarish, curved strokes and minimum stroke contrast.

Postmodern:
A plethora of these typefaces exist as a result of the digital revolution. These typefaces defy categorization.

CLASSIFICATION

An understanding of basic typeface classification is a fundamental prerequisite for making typeface selections. While it is nearly impossible to meaningfully classify the thousands of currently available typefaces, gaining a general overview of their historical development is a satisfactory starting point for making selections.

Old Style
Garamond

Transitional
Baskerville

Modern
Bodoni

Slab Serif
Serifa

Sanserif
Helvetica

postmodern
Variex

❶

❷

TYPEFACE DESIGN

As discussed in the previous section, legibility refers to qualities and attributes in typography that make type readable. Many factors contribute to legibility, such as interletter and interline spacing. But in the context of selecting typefaces, the first consideration is letterform design. Well-designed typefaces are open, clear, and consistent, and they exhibit no visual quirks,

a q a a

❸

a a a a

❹

Serif faces	Sanserif faces
Bembo	Franklin Gothic
Baskerville	Frutiger
Bodoni	Futura
Garamond	Gill Sans
Minion	Helvetica
Palatino	Optima
Times	Univers

❺

strange anomalies in shape, or meaningless decorative traits. They are medium in weight, not too heavy or too light, nor are they too narrow or too wide. In other words, there exists a visual balance between letter strokes and counterforms (the spaces within and around letters). Excellence in a typeface design is achieved when each of the letters of the alphabet is distinct from the next, and when

these diverse letters are visually unified through formal relationships. In other words, legibility is achieved by balancing unity and diversity.

2
For the exhibit *Shattering Notions*, Optima is used for heads and Serifa for subheads. Optima is a sanserif typeface with strokes terminating in a slight taper. Serifa possesses the optical qualities of Univers with the added feature of serifs for enhanced readability. (Exhibition: *Shattering Notions*, Christopher Chadbourne and Associates)

3
Four different typefaces possessing varying degrees of legibility.

4
Four different typefaces from the Frutiger family. Frutiger Roman (third from the left) is the most legible because of its medium weight.

5
Classical typefaces are timeless and distinct because of their shape and proportion. The features of classical typefaces are not exaggerated or overly pronounced, which might intrude upon readability.

6
Frutiger's characters are highly distinct, and the typeface possesses organic properties unlike many other sanserif typefaces. (Exhibition: Hancock Park, Sussman Prejza & Co. Inc.)

7
The highly legible Fenice, a serif face, is used for the body copy of this exhibition. (Exhibition: Hancock Park, Sussman Prejza & Co. Inc.)

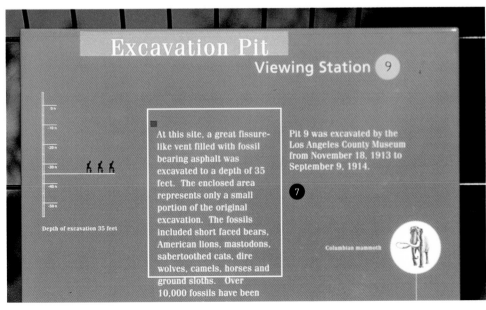

SHAPE OF THE UNIT. NONE "RAISES HIS VOICE" AT THE VISITOR – WHICH OFTEN HAPPENS WHEN SEPARATE BUT RELATED TEXTS ARE FORCED TO SHARE THE SAME SURFACE,

VERSATILITY

8

Type families vary in number of members, but the most versatile are those consisting of different weights and widths in both serif and sanserif varieties. Rotis, designed by the German designer, Otl Aicher in 1989, is one such example. This family also includes semisans and semiserif versions.

9

Expert fonts, which contain small capitals, ligatures, fractions, and other special characters, extend the capabilities of type families even further. Shown here are a few expert characters from Minion.

10

For this exhibit, the Futura family provides a spectrum of weights and widths, while maintaining formal unity and harmony. (Exhibition: *The Philips Competence Center*, The Burdick Group)

Versatile typefaces are those that are comfortable in a wide variety of situations and conditions. They possess the proportions of classical typefaces and they are members of a larger type family. A type family is the complete range of variations of a typeface design, including Roman, italic, bold, expanded, condensed, and special characters such as ligatures, and other characters that might be needed for mathematical data or foreign languages. Since the digital revolution, the range and size of type families have been greatly expanded with the introduction of multiple master typefaces and expert fonts. By interpolating between light and heavy, and condensed and expanded designs, a nearly unlimited palette of typographic expressions is accessible. Expert fonts are special font packages that expand the normal range of type families to include small capitals, fractions, and non-aligning numerals.

history
sanserif light

history
sanserif light italic

history
sanserif regular

history
sanserif regular italic

history
sanserif bold

history
sanserif extra bold

history
semisans light

history
semisans light italic

history
semisans regular

history
semisans regular italic

history
semisans bold

history
semisans extra bold

history
semiserif regular

history
semiserif bold

history
serif regular

history
serif regular italic

history
serif bold

8

ABCDEFGHI
JKLMNOPQ
RSTUVWXY
Z & ? $
1 2 3 4 5 6 7
8 9 0
¼ ½ ¾ ⅛
⅜ ⅝ ⅞ ⅓
⅔
Æ Œ ff ff fi
fl ffi ffl

10

By virtue of their visual characteristics (form, shape, and texture), typefaces are capable of suggesting moods and emotions, attitudes, historical periods, industries, and cultures. When considering typefaces for an exhibition, designers can take advantage of this communicative potential, establishing a fitting relationship between form and content. Each typeface must be carefully evaluated for its ability to suggest content, for even the most subtle trait or nuance can shift meaning.

Some serif typefaces are dignified, serious, and elegant. Sanserif typefaces appear more informal, and may be associated with simplicity and modernity. Typefaces possessing letters with unusual visual attributes such as odd or unusual proportions, angularity, roundness, narrowness, or heaviness can be exploited for their specific communication value.

11
The headlines appearing in the sturdy and mechanical typeface, Permanent Massive, suggest the technological theme of the exhibition. (Exhibition: *Possible Dreams: Popular Mechanics and America's Enthusiasm for Technology*, Staples & Charles Ltd)

12
Cooper Black, a funky American vernacular typeface, is brimful of musical energy and rhythm. (Exhibition: *I Want to Take You Higher*, Rock and Roll Hall of Fame and Museum, Pentagram)

13
Typefaces can visually reflect the meaning of the words and text they represent. Expressions range from subtle to obvious.

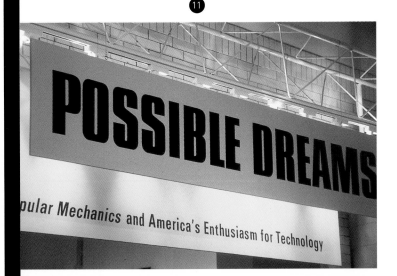

classical *jazz* blues

BLUEGRASS
rock and roll
techno

52

TYPOGRAPHIC RESONANCE

Typefaces serve as graphic symbols for sounds in spoken language. Beyond this critical role they also have the ability to resonate visually – to support, extend, or enhance underlying messages. Thus, typography is multidimensional; it is capable of communicating not only verbally, but visually and audibly as well. By virtue of their inherent visual characteristics, typefaces can suggest objects, images, and an array of sounds such as human speech, animal utterances, and music. Through their optical properties, they can set a tone, create a mood, emit an emotion. As the visual equivalent of spoken language, typefaces are capable of vividly referencing time periods and accurately transmitting information about culture.

14
Cereal boxes of different colors are used to form the word *Kellogg's* on this massive wall. Resonance factors are color, scale, and the unique method used. (Exhibition: *Kellogg's Cereal City USA*, Jack Rouse Associates)

15
Text set at angles on five acrylic panels suggests motion and space. Resonance factors: typographic structure and method of type application. (Exhibition: *American Airlines C.R. Smith Aviation Museum*, Zalisk Martin Associates Inc.)

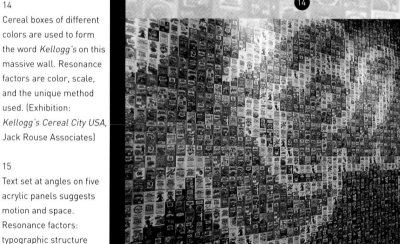

14

16

Photograph ©Ian McKinnell

15

Most often, when typography communicates on the visual level, it does so figuratively and metaphorically, not literally. In language, a metaphor is created by applying a name or descriptive term to a dissimilar object or action in a non-literal manner. In typography, this is accomplished by choosing suggestive typefaces, as well as by applying any number of formal variables to words and text, including shape, size, texture, direction, position, value, color, dimensionality, distortion, repetition, rhythm, exaggeration, and contrast. Manipulating typography figuratively can strengthen, augment, or support an exhibit's content. Also, the particular perspective desired by an exhibition's curators or developers can be significantly influenced by figurative typographic messages.

16
The word *LOOK* is combined with a huge casting of a human ear. Resonance factors: a three-dimensional ear is substituted for the word *HEAR*. (Exhibition: *Look Hear, Art and Science of the Ear*, Trickett & Webb Limited)

17
Spiraling outward from a flower suggesting the "flower power" movement of the 1960s, is multi-colored type presenting names of artists and music. Resonance factors: typographic structure, color, typeface, and theme. (Exhibition: *I Want to Take You Higher*, The Rock and Roll Hall of Fame, Pentagram)

18

Typography, images, and diagrams are presented on 6 x 10 foot theme panels made of film. Visitors are able to see through the panels to people moving around the exhibition. Resonance factors: scale, transparent material. (Exhibition: *Urban Revisions: Current Projects for the Public Realm*, April Greiman Associates)

When type effectively resonates, the audience for which it is intended is forced to pay attention, to contemplate, to respond empathetically. In exhibits, typography plays a formidable role in whether the experience is solidly imprinted in the memory, or whether the memory fades immediately upon leaving the exhibit site. Designers can employ specific mnemonic devices that optimize the potential for visitors to remember the exhibit experience. In addition to manipulating the visual elements of type (form, color, scale, texture, etc.), mnemonic factors may effectively include such tactics as lighting, supporting structures, projections, and sound.

18

19, 20
The participant is immersed in a multi-media experience of projected type and image, sound, moving type, and type positioned on walls and floor. The kiosk is constructed of seven curved screen panels. Resonance factors: projections, movement, sound. (Exhibition: *George Orwell's 1984*, Laura Mitchell)

21
For this trade show exhibit, the synthetic plastic material known as Corian is showcased as a large, free-standing wall of fragmented type in different Corian colors. Resonance factors: scale color, and presentation. (Exhibition: *Corian?, Corian!*, Pentagram)

OBSERVE FOR THEMSELVES THE SUCCESS OR FAILURE OF THE TYPOGRAPHIC PRESENTATION. ¶ FOR MOST GRAPHIC DESIGN STUDENTS, SEIZING THE OPPORTUNITIES

COMBINING TYPEFACES

22
Working with a type selection matrix can be an effective and time-saving method for selecting typeface combinations.

Contrast is the most important principle to consider:

serif/sanserif
functional/decorative
geometric/organic
bold/light
thick/thin
Roman/script
simple/complex

With rare exception, exhibits will utilize no more than two or three different typefaces. Using more than this number leads to visual chaos and a lack of order. Multiple typefaces are staged in exhibits to work as a team, but also to work individually in assigned roles. The most important consideration for selecting multiple typefaces is contrast, and variations in contrast are abundant: serif/sanserif, Roman/script, heavy/light, thick/thin, simple/ornamental. Plenty of contrast between typefaces ensures that each will effectively fulfill its task. Effective contrasts can also be achieved when using different typefaces within the same family, or using all capital letters in relationship to lowercase letters. There are no formulas when it comes to combining different typefaces. Judgement based on experience, an eye for contrast, and a concern for the exhibition's content all contribute to appropriate

	Baskerville	Bodoni	Garamond	
Arbitrary	Arbitrary Baskerville	Arbitrary Bodoni	Arbitrary Garamond	
Courier	Courier Baskerville	Courier Bodoni	Courier Garamond	
Franklin Gothic	Franklin Baskerville	Franklin Bodoni	Franklin Garamond	
Futura	Futura Baskerville	Futura Bodoni	Futura Garamond	
Meta	Meta Baskerville	Meta Bodoni	Meta Garamond	
Modula	Modula Baskerville	Modula Bodoni	Modula Garamond	
Rotis sans	Rotis sans Baskerville	Rotis sans Bodoni	Rotis sans Garamond	
Univers	univers Baskerville	univers Bodoni	univers Garamond	

selections. The process is one of physically comparing several combinations of type specimens until the best possibility emerges.

A systematic method for comparing typefaces is by means of a type selection matrix, as demonstrated below. The collection of typefaces shown in this matrix is classic, some are recommended by the Society for Environmental Graphic Design (SEGD), and based on the American with Disabilities Act

(ADA). While the matrix below compares only small specimens, it is important to compare specimens at different sizes, approximating as closely as possible type sizes as they will appear in an exhibition. It is also important to mention that this is a small sample matrix only. Every matrix will vary in scope, tailored to the needs of the specific project.

Minion	Palatino	Rotis serif	Serifa	Times
Arbitrary Minion	**Arbitrary** Palatino	**Arbitrary** Rotis serif	**Arbitrary** Serifa	**Arbitrary** Times
Courier Minion	Courier Palatino	Courier Rotis serif	Courier **Serifa**	Courier Times
Franklin Minion	Franklin Palatino	Franklin Rotis serif	Franklin **Serifa**	Franklin Times
Futura Minion	**Futura** Palatino	**Futura** Rotis serif	**Futura** Serifa	**Futura** Times
Meta Minion	Meta Palatino	Meta Rotis serif	Meta **Serifa**	Meta Times
Modula Minion	Modula Palatino	Modula Rotis serif	Modula **Serifa**	Modula Times
Rotis sans Minion	Rotis sans Palatino	Rotis sans Rotis serif	Rotis sans **Serifa**	Rotis sans Times
univers Minion	univers Palatino	univers Rotis serif	univers Serifa	univers Times

SPACE, MATERIALS, COLOR AND TEXTURE – AND ITS RELATIONSHIP TO TYPOGRAPHY. THEY DISCOVER THAT LIGHT AND LIGHTING ARE SIGNIFICANT COMPONENTS IN THE MIX.

STRUCTURE

To structure type is to organize typographic parts into a unified whole, and to establish a clear relationship between those parts. The ultimate goal of this endeavor is to make information as accessible as possible. Prior to making any decisions about the structuring of typographic elements, fundamental questions must be considered. Who is the audience? What is the purpose of the exhibition? What are the messages to be revealed? Upon answering these questions, the process begins with an analysis of the nature and complexity of the script (words that will accompany images, artifacts, and physical components). This analysis will enable the designer to determine a hierarchy between the components of the information, which must then be translated into appropriate spatial arrangements of typographic parts. Establishing an effective typographical hierarchy ensures that visitors are able to readily navigate an exhibition through a deliberate ordering of elements. Establishing hierarchical relationships is tied to the visual dynamics of similarity and contrast: parts sharing similar characteristics are more equal within the visual hierarchy; those having contrasting traits are either dominant or subordinate within the hierarchy. Contrast is achieved among typographical elements by means of size, weight, and color shifts, as well as by the spatial language of repetition, rhythm, and interval. Typographic grids are often used as an underlying framework for organizing and bringing spatial order to typographic elements.

LIGHTING DIMINISHES THE QUALITY OF THE EXPERIENCE. TODAY, GRAPHIC UNITS COMPETE WITH MONITORS FOR ATTENTION, AND I AM CONVINCED THAT THE APPEAL OF THE

STANDARD TYPE ALIGNMENTS

In exhibition design, unlike print, text type is unbounded by size, and the sizes used are largely determined by the readability of type at different viewing distances (see the foregoing section on legibility, and Chapter 3). Regardless, text alignments for exhibitions are identical to the standard configurations found in printed communications.

BALANCE

Two basic compositional schemes exist for structuring and organizing typographic elements in space: symmetry and asymmetry. Symmetrical structures are perceived as quiet and dignified, while asymmetrical organization is dynamic and assertive. Symmetry consists of type elements running bi-laterally along a centered axis; asymmetry derives its energy from the interaction of positive and negative spaces.

1

Illustrated from top to bottom are the standard type alignments: flush-left, ragged right; flush-right, ragged left; justified; centered (symmetrical); asymetrical.

2

This example of bi-lateral symmetry shows elements aligned on a centered axis (top). In asymmetrical balance, the axis is shifted to the left to create an active and varied division of space. Balance is derived from the interplay of positive and negative shapes (bottom).

Exhibition typography is like background music. Most people notice it only when it is noticeably bad. When it's good, typography calls less attention to itself than to the stories it's trying to tell, the mood it hopes to create, the content it seeks to express.

Exhibition typography is like background music. Most people notice it only when it is noticeably bad. When it's good, typography calls less attention to itself than to the stories it's trying to tell, the mood it hopes to create, the content it seeks to express.

Exhibition typography is like background music. Most people notice it only when it is noticeably bad. When it's good, typography calls less attention to itself than to the stories it's trying to tell, the mood it hopes to create, the content it seeks to express.

Exhibition typography is like background music. Most people notice it only when it is noticeably bad. When it's good, typography calls less attention to itself than to the stories it's trying to tell, the mood it hopes to create, the content it seeks to express.

Exhibition typography
　　　is like background music.
Most people notice it only
　　　　　when it is noticeably
bad.
　　　　　When it's good, typography

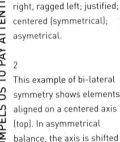

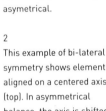

1

2

GROUPING

Typographic elements establish associations by being grouped together through their relative proximity, or by providing them with similar visual characteristics such as size, shape, weight, direction, color, etc. An expression of various degrees of separation and connection, or a strategic grouping of elements can aid visitors in navigating components of an exhibition by emphasizing some aspects and de-emphasizing others.

MACRO AND MICRO STRUCTURES

Structures in typographic space may also be observed in terms of the whole (macro), and in the part (micro). The essential relationship between macro and micro structures creates a synergetic spatial environment that is simultaneously simple and complex, and informative and visually engaging for visitors.

3
Grouping by color, weight, size, and typeface (left to right, top to bottom).

4
The two light units of text are grouped and the two dark units are grouped. Letters within the word *type* are also assigned different weights, expanding the number of corresponding parts.

5
The macro and micro structures of this exhibition panel are diagrammed to reveal a complex, layered typographic environment, and the relationship of the parts to the whole.

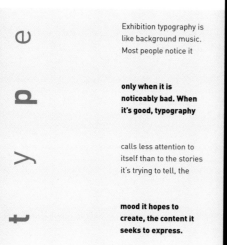

3

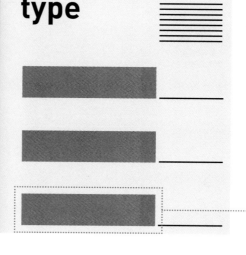

Exhibition typography is like background music. Most people notice it

only when it is noticeably bad. When it's good, typography

calls less attention to itself than to the stories it's trying to tell, the

mood it hopes to create, the content it seeks to express.

4

5

6

When aligning type, it is very helpful to imagine the typographic units as solid geometric shapes, and aligning these shapes at the edges. Notice that the small round form is aligned at its center to the meanline of the adjacent text (top).

Making subtle optical adjustments when aligning type units is crucially important. Notice that the meanline of the word *type* aligns with the baseline of the adjacent headline, and that the baseline of the same word aligns with the meanline of the adjacent text. A slight optical adjustment was made by allowing the rounded strokes of the word *type* to extend above and below the horizontal alignments (bottom).

7

Effective hierarchies among typographic parts can be established by assigning appropriate visual characteristics to the parts. Shown in this example are six variables that can be employed sin-gularly or in combination as appropriate.

Spatial interval:
Elements can be separated from each other to emphasize distinct parts.

Weight:
Elements appearing heavier or lighter than other elements can appear more or less dominant because of their visual separation.

COMPOSITIONAL ALIGNMENT

Because type is geometric in nature, possessing internal structures (strokes) that are adamantly horizontal, vertical, and diagonal, typographical elements can achieve structural integrity by means of visual alignments. Because working with type is an optical process, and not purely mechanical, optical adjustments must be made to ensure proper alignments.

VISUAL HIERARCHY

Visual hierarchy refers to an ordering of parts that establish patterns not unlike those found in nature and the arts. A conch shell and tree branch exhibit ordered patterns, as do the analogous color relationships observed in paintings by Monet and Cézanne. Typographical hierarchy is established when each constituent part finds a relationship with every other part, contributing to a unified

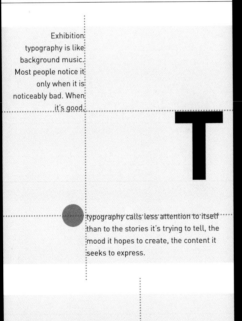

Exhibition typography is like background music. Most people notice it only when it is noticeably bad. When it's good

T

typography calls less attention to itself than to the stories it's trying to tell, the mood it hopes to create, the content it seeks to express.

type

Exhibition typography

Exhibition typography is like background music. Most people notice it only when it is noticeably bad. When it's good, typography calls less attention to itself than to the stories it's trying to tell, the mood it hopes to create, the content it seeks to express.

type

Exhibition typography is like background music. Most people notice it only when it is noticeably bad. When it's good, typography calls less attention to itself than to the stories it's trying to tell, the mood it hopes to create, the content it seeks to express.

t y p e

Exhibition typography is like background music. Most people notice it only when it is noticeably bad. When it's good, typography calls less attention to itself than to the stories it's trying to tell, the mood it hopes to create, the content it seeks to express.

Exhibition typography is like background music. Most people notice it only when it is noticeably bad. When it's good, typography calls less attention to itself than to the stories it's trying to tell, the mood it hopes to create, the content it seeks to express.

type

Exhibition typography is like background music.

Most people notice it only when it is noticeably bad.

When it's good, typography calls less attention to itself than to the stories it's trying to tell, the mood it hopes to create, the content it seeks to express.

type

Exhibition typography is like background music. Most people notice it only when it is noticeably bad. When it's good, typography calls less attention to itself than to the stories it's trying to tell, the mood it hopes to create, the content it seeks to express.

spatial interval

type
Exhibition typography is like background music. Most people notice it only when it is noticeably bad. When it's good, typography calls less attention to itself than to the stories it's trying to tell, the mood it hopes to create, the content it seeks to express.

type

Exhibition typography is like background music. Most people notice it only when it is noticeably bad. When it's good, typography calls less attention to itself than to the stories it's trying to tell, the mood it hopes to create, the content it seeks to express.

type

Exhibition typography is like background music. **Most people notice it only when it is noticeably bad.** When it's good, typography calls less attention to itself than to the stories it's trying to tell, the mood it hopes to create, the content it seeks to express.

type **Exhibition typography is like background music.** Most people notice it only when it is noticeably bad.

When it's good, typography calls less attention to itself than to the stories it's trying to tell, the mood it hopes to create, the content it seeks to express.

weight

whole. We perceive these hierarchical patterns as both message carriers and rhythmic visual structures, and they are most often perceived as a gradational series governed by laws of similarity and contrast. A gradational series can be expressed as a series of visual relationships, i.e., large to small, dark to light, or blue to yellow. To establish clear

hierarchical relationships, the distinctions among the parts must be deliberate and unambiguous.

Size:
The variable of size is perhaps the most obvious way of emphasizing one element in relationship to other elements.

Direction:
The physical direction in which typographic elements appear to be moving can add emphasis.

Typeface:
Because different typefaces vary in shape and proportion, emphasis can be achieved by juxtaposing one typeface with another. Introducing too many typefaces, however, can be confusing, since clear and simple visual distinctions are muddied.

Color:
Introducing color (as well as value contrasts) is a highly effective way to achieve hierarchical emphasis. The more contrast among colors, the more distinction among elements.

size

direction

typeface

color

In typographic design, elements are perceived as standing either in opposition or correspondence. When elements are in correspondence they are repeated; when in opposition, they stand in contrast to one another. The interplay of opposing and corresponding elements creates rhythmic structures not unlike those found in music. The basic structural pattern in music is expressed as statement-departure-return (ABA). The richly varied patterns arising from ABA typographic structures reveal the carefully planned order and emphasis of typographic elements, and provide visual variety that stimulates the eye and mind of the visitor. Typographic rhythms are composed with the aid of a typographic grid, an underlying organizational framework.

8

The identical size and weight of the heads *A* establish them as related elements. The two contrasting text blocks *B* are also linked together visually (top).

Although the small text block and the photograph *B* function differently on the panel, their size connects them together (middle).

The ABA structures observed in this simulation of a graphic rail give order and emphasis to the heads, text, photographs, and timeline (bottom).

Exhibition Exhibition typography is like background music. Most people notice it only when it is noticeably bad. When it's good, typography calls less attention to itself than to the stories it's trying to tell, the mood it hopes to create, the content it seeks to express.

| A | B |

Typography Exhibition typography is like background music. Most people notice it only when it is noticeably bad. When it's good, typography calls less attention to itself than to the stories it's trying to tell, the mood it hopes to create, the content it seeks to express.

| A | B |

Exhibition typography is like background music. Most people notice it only when it is noticeably bad. When it's good, typography calls less attention to itself than to the stories it's trying to tell, the mood it hopes to create, the content it seeks to express.

Exhibition typography is like background music. Most people notice it only when it's good, typography calls less attention to itself than to the stories it's trying to tell, the mood it hopes to create, the content it seeks to express.

| A | B |

Exhibition typography is like background music. Most people notice it only when it is noticeably bad. When it's good, typography calls less attention to itself than to the stories it's trying to tell, the mood it hopes to create, the content it seeks to express.

| A | B |

Exhibition

Exhibition typography is like background music. Most people notice it only when it is noticeably bad. When it's good, typography calls less attention to itself than to the stories it's trying to tell, the mood it hopes to create, the content it seeks to express.

Typography

Exhibition typography is like background music. Most people notice it only when it is noticeably bad. When it's good, typography calls less attention to itself than to the stories it's trying to tell, the mood it hopes to create, the content it seeks to express.

| 1000 | 1100 | 1200 | 1300 | 1400 | 1500 | 1600 | 1700 |

Exhibition

Exhibition typography is like background music. Most people notice it only when it is noticeably bad. When it's good, typography calls less attention to itself than to the stories it's trying to tell, the mood it hopes to create, the content it seeks to express.

Typography

Exhibition typography is like background music. Most people notice it only when it is noticeably bad. When it's good, typography calls less attention to itself than to the stories it's trying to tell, the mood it hopes to create, the content it seeks to express.

| A | B | A | B |

GRIDS

A typographic grid possesses specific features related to the unique physical requirements of typographic layout, and is an invaluable aid in organizing typography and other visual elements. Grid features include margins, which provide consistent boundaries for all layout elements; vertical columns with intervals separating them for text type; grid modules used to govern the placement of type and image; flow lines that enable alignment of elements from one design component (such as an exhibition panel) to another; and spatial zones (connected grid modules) that are reserved for the placement of specific content, whether type or image. Determining the exact proportions and complexity of grids, and how to employ them is based upon the nature of the content, legibility concerns, and desired visual effects.

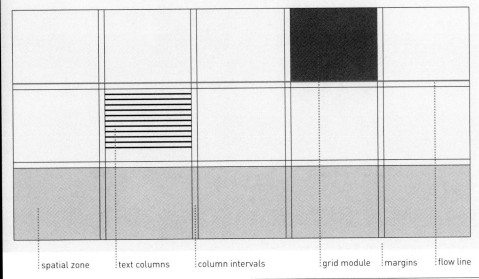

| spatial zone | text columns | column intervals | grid module | margins | flow line |

9

Typographic grids are designed to best accommodate content (heads, text, photographs, illustrations, diagrams, and other exhibition components). Each grid is configured in response to the specific hierarchical requirements of the content (top).

Grids range in complexity and modular variations. It is the designer's task to transform this rigid framework into a rhythmic and communicative layout (bottom).

Exhibition Typography

Exhibition typography is like background music. Most people notice it only when it is noticeably bad. When it's good, typography calls less attention to itself than to the stories it's trying to tell, the mood it hopes to create, the content it seeks to express.

Exhibition typography is like background music. Most people notice it only when it is noticeably bad. When it's good, typography calls less attention to itself than to the stories it's trying to tell, the mood it hopes to create, the content it seeks to express.

Exhibition Typography

Exhibition typography is like background music. Most people notice it only when it is noticeably bad. When it's good, typography calls less attention to itself than to the stories it's trying to tell, the mood it hopes to create, the content it seeks to express.

Exhibition Typography

Exhibition typography is like background music. Most people notice it only when it is noticeably bad. When it's good, typography calls less attention to itself than to the stories it's trying to tell, the mood it hopes to create, the content it seeks to express.

grid variations

SPECIAL CONSIDERATIONS

The role of exhibitions has evolved dramatically in recent years due to changing expectations of visitors, and a rush of new technologies effecting all aspects of the communications industry. In response to the widening diversity of visitors, exhibit developers are embracing a philosophy that is inclusive rather than exclusive, open rather than closed. Messages voiced by exhibitions are crossing cultural and sociological boundaries. Regardless of age, gender, race, social class, or physical status, the democratic nature of exhibitions mandates impartiality. In the realm of exhibitions, typography continues to serve as a teacher, a mediator, and a guide. But in the changing face of exhibition culture, these roles must be reconsidered and redefined. If thoughtfully considered, typography can make the exhibition experience more equitable and more accessible to more people. It can respond effectively to the needs of a multilingual audience, help visitors more effectively navigate exhibit spaces, and enable them to absorb meaningful information regardless of how it is organized. Typography is a tool capable of not only informing visitors, but of also challenging them to think more broadly about historical and contemporary issues.

PRESENTATION ORIGINATED. THE ACTORS ARE NOT ENGAGED WITH THE AUDIENCE SO MUCH AS WITH THE SCENERY, MUSIC, AND COSTUMES THAT CREATE THE EFFECT OF

MULTILINGUAL EXHIBITS

When working with typography in multilingual exhibits, designers should keep in mind that texts will change in length depending upon the languages represented, and the relative accuracy of the translations. Special consideration should also be given to the hierarchy of one language text in relationship to another, for even subtle changes in typographic treatment can change emphasis. To avoid partiality and subtle miscommunication, texts of different languages should be treated the same. Where languages do require emphasis over others, criteria should exist for making such distinctions.

1

When working with multiple language exhibits, it can be assumed that translated texts will differ in length by about 10 – 30%, depending upon the languages and the manner in which they are translated. The same text set in Spanish and English is longer in Spanish because the text is composed of more words.

2

Individual words are longer in some languages than in others because they are composed of more characters. Thus more space is required when set into type.

3

These reader rails present German text in Sabon and the English translation in Syntax. The German is positioned above the English text, as the majority of visitors to this exhibition speak German. (Exhibition: *Zum Schutz des Landes*, *(In Defense of Styria)*, Staples & Charles Ltd)

The First Farmer
3,000 years ago

New Mexico's first farmer was probably a woman born in a community in present-day Mexico. Her home community had recently started growing crops to supplement their hunting and gathering lifestyle. In the tradition of her ancestors she joined a different hunter-gatherer group as a young woman – perhaps as part of an exchange of goods and people. She brought the knowledge of domesticated plants to New Mexico with her.

English / 75 words

El primer labrador
Hace 3,000 años

El primer labriego de Nuevo México fue probablemente una mujer nacida en una comunidad en lo que hoy es México. Su comunidad comenzó recientemente a cultivar hortalizas para complementar su estilo de vida de cacería y recolecta. Según la tradición de sus antepasados, ella se unió durante su juventud a diferentes grupos de cazadores y recolectores – tal vez como parte de un intercambio de géneros y gente. Ella trajo consigo a Nuevo México el conocimiento de las plantas domesticadas.

Spanish / 84 words

1

Choosing typefaces

The first step in making type legible is to choose text typefaces that are open and well proportioned. Typefaces that exhibit the regularity of classical serif faces such as Baskerville, Bembo, Bodoni, Garamond; and the sans serif faces Franklin Gothic, Frutiger, and Gill Sans. Typefaces with visual quirks, stylistic affectations, and irregularities among characters are less legible. Typefaces such as these may be fine, however, when used as display type.

English / 72 words

Schriftenauswahl

Der erste Schritt, um den SchriDsatz besser lesbar zu gestalten, ist die Wahl von Textschriften, die offen und wohl proportioniert sind, z. B. Schriften mit der Regelmalligkeit klassischer Antiquaschriften wie die Baskerville, Bembo, Bodoni' Garamond; und die Groteskschriffen (Sans Serif) Franklin Gothic, Frutiger und Gill Sans. Schriffen mit visuellen Schnorkeln, stilistischer Affektiertheit und Unregelmalligkeiten zwischen Buchstaben sind schlechter lesbar. Solche Schriffen konnen andererseits jedoch fur Uberschriffen als Display-Schriffen sehr brauchbar sein.

German / 73 words

2

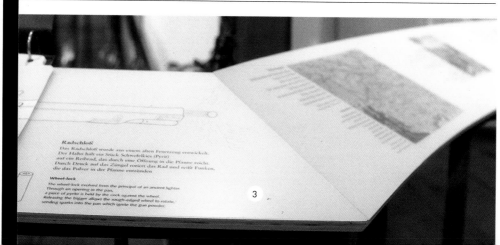

THE "OTHER WORLD" INSIDE THE FRAME. DIORAMA DESIGN ACCOMPLISHES THE SAME GOAL. AQUARIUM DESIGN, AND ARTIFACT CASES CAN ALSO GIVE US THE SENSE OF

3

④

De collectie Van Velzen
Liefdewerk oud papier

For the Love of Days Gone By
The Van Velzen Collection

Wat hebben een matze-stoffertje, een collectebusje voor De Joodsche Blinde en een grammofoonplaat van Johnny and Jones met elkaar gemeen? Ze maken alle deel uit van de waardevolle collectie Van Velzen over het Nederlandse joodse leven. Recent is deze verzameling aan de collectie van het Joods Historisch Museum toegevoegd. De tentoonstelling presenteert een eerste keuze uit het omvangrijke materiaal dat meer dan vierduizend stuks omvat. 'Verzamelen wat er niet meer was' stond Van Velzen voor ogen. In dertig jaar heeft hij ruim drie eeuwen joods leven in Nederland teruggehaald. Dingen die alledaags en betekenisloos leken, zijn bijeengebracht en geven samen een beeld van dat wat verdwenen is.

What do a brush for mazzah crumbs, a money-box for De Joodsche Blinde and a Johnny and Jones phonograph record have in common? They all come from Van Velzen's valuable collection about Jewish life in the Netherlands. Recently this collection was added to that of the Jewish Historical Museum. The exhibition features a choice selection from the vast material comprising over four thousand items. Van Velzen aimed to 'collect what was no more'. In three decades he retrieved over three centuries of Jewish life in the Netherlands. Things that appeared mundane and trivial are gathered to offer an overall impression of what has disappeared.

⑤

Alle landen
All countries

Alle landen
All countries

Alle landen
All countries

Alle landen
All countries

Alle landen
All countries

Alle landen
All countries

4
This detail of an introductory panel features both Dutch and English. The typeface and size of type are the same for the two languages, giving each equal prominence. However, because Dutch is the primary language of visitors, it precedes English and is graphically separated by a ruled line. (Exhibition: *For the Love of Days Gone By*, Marit van der Meer and Josephine Oudijn)

5
Changing the face, weight, color, or posture of type can affect the emphasis given to multilingual elements. This is especially important when considering wayfinding and signage.

TACTILE TYPOGRAPHY AND BRAILLE

Designers should be familiar with the use of tactile typography and Braille and how these forms can be effectively integrated either together or separately into exhibits. Tactile letters should be raised a minimum of 1/32", and they should be sized between 5/8" to 2" high.

Two grades of Braille are available, and both are basically the same, with the exception that Grade 2 Braille offers additional characters and character combinations representing certain words and word components. Because of these added attributes, Grade 2 Braille is recommended over Grade 1 Braille.

Braille exists in only one size, and is read with the flat pad of the finger, not the tip. In the exhibit setting, Braille should never be placed too close to other raised surfaces such as relief letters and decorative frames. These may obstruct the Braille and prevent it from being read correctly. When producing Braille, care should be taken that the raised dots are smooth and rounded rather than sharp and cylindrical; the tactile patterns should be easily distinguished by the scanning finger.

6

When Braille is used, it should be predictably and consistently applied to exhibition components such as signs, graphic rails and graphic panels. In addition, these exhibit components should be strategically located so that they are easily accessible to visitors both in and out of wheelchairs. When the application of Braille is a design requirement, it should be considered early in the design process. (Exhibition: Museé des Beaux Arts Calais, Coco Raynes Associates, Inc.)

7

Braille on plastic strips can be hidden along the inner surfaces of handrails for easy access to blind visitors. (Coco Raynes Associates, Inc.)

8

Raised typography appears on a graphic rail alongside Braille. These elements are raised on sandblasted tempered glass, a process that yields superb typographic clarity. (Exhibition: Museé des Beaux Arts Calais, Coco Raynes Associates, Inc.)

For complete information regarding the use of Braille and to order the BrailleFont program disk, contact the Society of Environmental Graphic Design (SEGD), whose address and telephone number are located in the back of this book.

6

Auguste Rodin
Paris 1840 - Meudon 1917
Les Bourgeois de Calais - 1885
Deuxième maquette pour le Monument

Bronze. Fonte Susse, 1973
Dépôt du Musée Rodin, 1973
D.77.5.1

7

Auguste Rodin
Paris 1840 - Meudon 1917

Tête d'Eustache de Saint-Pierre
Etude pour le Monument
des Bourgeois de Calais - Vers 1886-1887

Bronze. Fonte E. Godard, 1981
Don des Amis du Musée de Calais, 1981
81.13.1

Photograph ©Bill Miles

8

TACTILE IMAGES

To enrich the museum experience for people who are visually impaired, selected images and artifacts found in exhibits can be represented as simplified raised outlines. This requires a careful translation and reduction of images, a process of isolating only the most pronounced and relevant aspects. Superfluous visual information only confuses visitors. Like typography, the raised contours should be distinct and raised to an optimum height of 1/32".

9, 10
A painting has been carefully translated into its most essential form, enabling a visually impaired visitor to experience it through touch. (Exhibition: Museo Nacional de Colombia, Coco Raynes Associates, Inc.)

9

10

ILLUMINATION, AND HOW TO MAKE IT LEGIBLE IN DIMLY LIT SPACE. ¶ ANOTHER WAY STUDENTS SHOULD BE COMPELLED TO LOOK AT TYPOGRAPHY IS AS "INTRUSION." THERE

11
By means of numerals within yellow circles, visitors are clearly informed about the locations of specific attractions. (Exhibition: Hancock Park, Sussman/Prejza & Co. Inc.)

12
A large title wall directs visitors to the starting point of an exhibit. Smaller wayfinding signs establish visitor pathways. (Exhibition: Liberty Science Center, Donovan and Green)

13, 14
An excellent example of immersion, the physical structure of this exhibit suggests a flower, a powerful icon of the 1960s. The center of the "flower" is the spatial core of the exhibit, with the "petals," serving as thematic exhibit spaces. With the support of typography and rich color, this exhibit vividly immerses visitors into its content. (Exhibition: *I Want to Take You Higher*, Rock and Roll Hall of Fame and Museum, Pentagram)

VISITOR CIRCULATION

The design of exhibitions is based upon a synergetic relationship between content, form, and function (use). Decisions regarding any one of these important aspects is dependent also upon the others. The form of an exhibit, for example, is directly related to its established content, and how an audience physically negotiates an exhibit is tied ultimately to its form. Visitor circulation may therefore be a random process, or it may be based upon a carefully articulated system of movement.

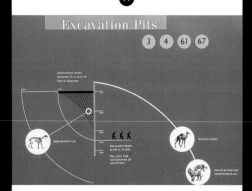

11

©Wolfgang Hoyt, Photographer

12

IMMERSION

Immersion occurs when visitors physically, mentally, and/or emotionally leave the reality of their daily lives and are absorbed into the content of an exhibition and how it is presented. When immersed, visitors can feel lost, frustrated, challenged, emotional, curious, or intellectually heightened. Always, there exists an empathic response between the visitor and what is visited, and the experience remains cemented in the memory. Typography is often the bridge to this poignant transformation.

13

14

ILLUMINATION

Illumination is a key to preserving typographic legibility, establishing visual hierarchy, and creating drama. Strategic lighting can bring life to spaces and objects, and set the tone for an entire exhibit. Modulating space by means of the interplay between light and shadow creates a rhythmic and magical atmosphere. Both ambient and directed light should be considered for optimum lighting effectiveness. In situations where ambient light is too dim, carefully directed light is necessary to ensure typographic legibility and visual fidelity.

©Wolfgang Hoyt, Photographer

15
In dimly lit spaces, spot lights precisely illuminate their subjects and provide visual drama. (Exhibition: Liberty Science Center, Donovan and Green)

16
In this covered exhibition space, ambient outdoor light effectively illuminates graphic panels and kiosks. (Exhibition: *Grasslands*, Main Street Design, Inc.)

©Hoachlander – Davis Photography

WHERE SILENCE IS THOROUGHLY APPROPRIATE, OR A WHISPER IS AS LOUD AS A MESSAGE SHOULD BE. A GOOD EXAMPLE OF THIS IS THE SNOW MONKEYS EXHIBIT AT THE

CENTRAL PARK ZOO. THE NEW YORK ZOOLOGICAL SOCIETY HAS GONE TO ENORMOUS EFFORT TO CREATE THE ILLUSION FOR THE VISITOR THAT HE SHARES THE SNOW

READABLE LABELS:
THE PERCEIVED CONFLICT
BETWEEN FORM
AND FUNCTION

ESSAY BY JANICE MAJEWSKI

MONKEY'S NATURAL HABITAT. THE EXHIBIT IS FLOODED BY NATURAL LIGHT. WHAT PURPOSE HERE, THE GRAPHIC DESIGNER MIGHT ASK, WOULD A BIG PIECE OF IDENTITY

Janice Majewski is
Coordinator of
Smithsonian Accessibility
of the Accessibility
Program at the
Smithsonian Institution
Washington, DC

A frequent complaint from museum visitors is that they cannot read exhibit labels. These voices of frustration come from a varied group of individuals: some are legally blind, many have changes in vision due to age, a few have dyslexia, and some are just the victims of cutting-edge graphic design. Whatever the particular reason for their inability to read the text, the result is the same: the desired information is not received. And often, type – linked with co-conspirators such as limited color contrast and low lighting – is at fault.

GRAPHICS SERVE? A GOOD QUESTION, ELEGANTLY ANSWERED BY A SIMPLE HANDRAIL GRAPHIC MEASURING NO MORE THAN 4 X 12 INCHES. IN THIS INSTANCE, THE VISITOR'S

Why worry whether signs and labels are accessible to a diverse public? A major reason is the fact that the world's population is aging. And with age come the common companions of vision loss due to cataracts, macular degeneration, and worsening farsightedness, among others. An exhibit designer once said that museums do not have to advocate for accessibility, they simply should hire older designers. For with older designers, museums get larger, clearer, more readable type, and everyone – including the creators of the labels – can read it. A high percentage of museum visitors today are older adults; in the next 30 years, the percentage is predicted to increase dramatically. If exhibit labels are not accessible to this audience, there will be few people remaining to read them.

This is not to say that there is a formula for developing labels that accommodate everyone all of the time. There is, of course, no one-size-fits-all in design; the aim is, instead, solutions that are one-size-fits-many. And, there are almost as many solutions as there are variables, so each recipe is unique and based on the individual exhibit's characteristics.

age 90   age 80   age 70   age 60

1
Larger type does not necessarily translate into "clunky" type. The key is to adjust the proportions of all exhibit components into a harmonious whole. Most people appreciate exhibit type that is large enough to compensate for diminished vision or reading disabilities.

age 50   age 40   age 30   age 20

age 15   age 10   age 8   age 5

RELATIONSHIP TO THE TYPOGRAPHIC MESSAGE IS VERY INTIMATE, AND I WOULD VENTURE TO SAY, RESPECTFUL. THE HIERARCHY IS CLEAR; THE VISITOR'S PRIMARY

EXPERIENCE IS THE IMMEDIATE ENVIRONMENT WHICH IS ITSELF EXCEEDINGLY RICH WITH INFORMATION, PLANT MATERIAL, MOVEMENT, AND SOUND. ¶ STUDENTS NEED TO

2
Typefaces and chairs have much in common. A novelty typeface may have a temporary allure, but this does not translate into readability. A decorative chair may appear more comfortable, but bells and whistles only mask its true function, which is simply to be sat in. A careful consideration of the needs of the audience will reveal the most appropriate typeface and type size.

3
For people with vision loss, type with extreme thick and thin strokes can be a problem, as thin strokes disappear, leaving only remnants of the actual letterforms. Typefaces with minimum contrast in stroke widths are most readable.

4
Examples of type that should be avoided for use as text, particularly in large amounts: novelty typefaces, italics, scripts, typefaces that are too heavy, light, condensed, or expanded.

5
Stretching type with the aid of a computer should be avoided, as the correct proportions of the letterforms are distorted.

Much of what is being produced currently in the area of accessible text is heavily dependent on the creativity and knowledge of the designer, with the most successful designers being those who are open to the ideas that form and function are equally essential in a product and that accessible, attractive type is not an oxymoron. These are the designers who can see past the myth that access limits choices to the more accurate truth that access only changes choices.

If there are no foolproof formulas for accessible labels and sign text, then what's a designer to do? The first requirement is to listen to the audience members and consider the difficulties they face with type. Characteristics that make type particularly difficult to read include the following:

Type that is too small or too light and or has unequal stroke widths, with "thins" that for the reader disappear, or look like fly specks instead of print. Thin, lightweight strokes can break or vanish for people with vision loss, presenting only partial letterforms to decode.

2

type
type
type

3

Exhibition typogra
it only when it is n
attention to itself
hopes to create, th

Type that is ornate, set in italic or oblique, or imitates script or calligraphy distorts word shapes and makes individual letters impossible to discern.

Spacing presents problems when there is insufficient kerning or leading, right justification or centering, or excessively long lines. Each of these spacing issues can prevent someone with vision loss or learning disability from discriminating individual words, maintaining comprehension all through a line of type, and following sentences from line to line.

There are also problematic design choices that have the capability to sink or save the readability of type. Even the most accessible typefaces – such as Helvetica, Univers, and Futura – can be made inaccessible by these and other conditions:

Contrast, contrast, contrast (the absolute key with which many with low vision open visual mysteries). Without sufficient contrast (the Americans with Disabilities Act – the ADA – currently recommends a 70% contrast, based

6
In printed communications, text type ranges in point size from 6 to 11 *a*, while in exhibitions it ranges between 24 to 60 and beyond *b*. As type increases in size, so does the space surrounding it. Thus, consistent spacing between letters, words, and lines is all the more critical.

7
This is an excellent example of exhibition text set with optimum readability in mind. The letter, word, and line spacing, and the length of the lines demonstrate proportional harmony.

type / **type** *type* / type *type* / **type**

④

stretch / stretch

⑤

a   b

⑥

s like background music. Most people notice ably bad. When it's good, typography calls less o the stories it's trying to tell, the mood it ntent it seeks to express.

⑦

on light reflectance values), type disappears into its background and becomes nonexistent for the viewer.

Print-on-print is rarely readable by those with vision loss or learning disability. The problems are color contrast and competition. The degree of color contrast changes with each section of the print, making the levels vary constantly. The print also competes visually with the type making people who have visual perceptual difficulties stop, lose track of words, and often give up due to frustration.

Shiny surface qualities of materials – such as glossy Plexiglas or coated paper stock – on which the type is printed reflects light, causing glare. Glare for people with visual impairments, caused by such conditions as cataracts, blots out everything in the area of the reflection, making reading impossible.

Lighting, when it's poor quality, or there's not enough, or it's poorly directed and causing glare or shadows, eradicates the ability to read. Lighting, like color contrast, is key for people with vision loss or specific learning disabilities. Good quality light, without

8

The contrast between type and its background is a matter of value relationships. Black on white and white on black offer the most contrast. When using color with type, value contrast is a more important consideration than hue.

9

Type-on-type provides intriguing visual textures, but is rarely readable. The broken and uneven background of the bottom layer of type disturbs the continuity of the letterforms forming the top layer.

30% contrast

50% contrast

70% contrast

100% contrast

Exhibition typography is like background music. Most people notice it only when it is noticeably bad. When it's good, typography calls less attention to itself than to the stories it's trying to tell, the mood it hopes to create, the content it seeks to express.

8

9

substantial glare or shadow, should be provided at levels between 10 footcandles and 30 footcandles (100 – 300 lux) on and around labels.

The angle and distance of viewing can make the most accessible label totally inaccessible. People with vision loss often have short fields of vision. This means that labels at the back of two-foot deep cases can be out of range, depending on type size and color contrast.

Page organization and white space are both essential for people who have difficulty tracking type, who are daunted by heavy blocks of type, or have difficulty following one line to the next. Organized blocks of type help people find the beginning of a paragraph and follow the framework to the end of a text. If the lines are too long or if the label is filled with type, people who read word by word with difficulty will be stopped in frustration before they even start.

type

type

type

type

type

type

type

type

Exhibition typography is like background music. Most people notice it only when it is noticeably bad. When it's good, typography calls less attention to itself than to the stories it's trying to tell, the mood it hopes to create, the content it seeks to express. Exhibition typography is like background music. Most people notice it only when it is noticeably bad. When it's good, typography calls less attention to itself than to the stories it's trying to tell, the mood it hopes to create, the content it seeks to express. Exhibition typography is like background music. Most people notice it only when it is noticeably bad. When it's good,

Exhibition typography is like background music. Most people notice it only when it is noticeably bad. When it's good, typography calls less attention to itself than to the stories it's trying to tell, the mood it hopes to create, the content it seeks to express.

10
Generally, the smaller the type, the darker in value it must be against its background to be optimally readable.

11
Think of white space not as "wasted space," but as visual mortar that separates visual parts within a spatial field, establishes a logical visual hierarchy, and facilitates compositional integrity and beauty.

10

 11

TYPOGRAPHY ARE AFFECTED BY SCALE. SO THEY NEED A GOOD, SOLID SENSE OF THE TECHNICAL DEMANDS MADE ON TYPOGRAPHY IN THE EXHIBIT CONTEXT. THESE ARE

This is a daunting list of variables and inclusive of some of the most favored design elements today. What's left? Almost everything, if features are used with consideration and with a willingness to eliminate – on a case-by-case basis – what fails the tests of function.

It is difficult, if not impossible, to create a list of "accessibility compliant" fonts. Some typefaces work sufficiently well when they are large and heavy but fail miserably when they drop below a particular type size. Others work well when printed in dark on light combinations but become illegible when printed light on dark. The best advice is to employ fonts like Helvetica and Univers along with Century School Book as reference types. These faces have, over the years, continued to satisfy requirements for a large number of people. Judge other typefaces against them to determine if your choices will suit your specific

12

A pair of words composed of sanserif letters, and a pair of words composed of serif letters reveal how legibility can diminish in type with heavy strokes and small counters, or in type with extreme contrast in letter strokes.

13

Examples of serif and sanserif typefaces. The highlighted faces are sturdy models of functional clarity. The non-highlighted examples are popular typefaces possessing mild eccentricities that nonetheless compromise their performance as readable forms.

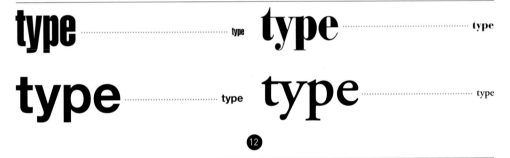

12

13

project. You can also gauge your type choices against the features listed earlier along with the following accessibility characteristics.

Typefaces that work for people with vision loss are mainly those with a large x-height, consistent stroke width, and clean lines, primarily but not solely sanserif fonts.

Extenders – above and below the line – must be sufficient to readily differentiate *p* from *b* from *o*, and *h* from *n*.

Numbers present much confusion: good fonts have *3, 8, 5,* and *6* all easily distinguishable from each other.

Medium weights often work best as lightweight fonts can break or disappear while extra bold face lowercase letters often fill in visually to become ink blobs (e.g., *e* versus *e*).

To confuse the issue slightly, everything changes, however, when discussion shifts to tactile characters – type read by touch. With tactile characters (raised a minimum of 1/32"),

14
X-height is a term used to describe the distance between the baseline and meanline of type. Not all typefaces of the same size have the same x-height. For people with vision loss, the larger the x-height the better.

15
As illustrated in this example, inadequate ascenders and descenders make it difficult to differentiate certain letters (top and middle). The letter *e* can be confused with the letter *o* if the curved stroke is not sufficiently open (bottom).

16
Numerals in the top example appear to be more easily distinguishable from one another than in the middle example. Both examples, however, provide clarity among numerals. Numerals such as those in the bottom example are easily confused.

accessible design calls for thin lines, all uppercase letters, absolutely nothing but sanserif faces, and heights between 1/2" and 3/4". However, tactile characters are only required in limited areas in buildings and only for permanent room identification. Signs with tactile characters and Braille must be located in very predictable locations so that people who are blind do not have to search the walls to find the signage. (The ADA currently requires that permanent room identification is located on the latch side of the door at 60" to the centerline of the sign.)

Whether text is read visually or tactually, the most valuable tip in deciding the accessibility of exhibit type is to prototype the labels and test them with older adults and people who are blind or have low vision. If the text works for these visitors, it is likely to work for everyone.

17
Tactile characters and Braille should be consistently and predictably placed within components of an exhibit to ensure ease of access. (Museo Nacional de Colombia, Coco Raynes Associates, Inc.)

Conclusion

Accessibility is not something about which to become discouraged. To paraphrase the old adage: "We are given accessibility issues to challenge us, not to destroy us." The creative effort is to find those "wow" solutions that are readable by almost everyone. If people look at your cutting-edge design and hesitate once or twice because they struggle to decipher the words or lose track of a line, they are likely to give up and quit reading. But that doesn't mean that they have to be bored visually while reading it either. A multitude of choices lies between those two eventualities. There is tremendous need for research in this area, to discover the parameters of readability for a diverse group of abilities and to decide how far those boundaries can be pushed. The challenge, then, is for designers to recognize that the medium is not always the message; in fact, the medium can fog or eliminate the message. The text is the message. How do we use the media to convey it effectively?

18
The objective of this installation was to increase awareness of the 75th Anniversary of the 19th Amendment given a small budget and an enormous room. By enlarging the law to fill the space, passersby were confronted with the monumental one-sentence amendment – 28 revolutionary words that were fought over for 70 years. The text was applied in eight foot letters (9,936 point type) to the marble floors. (*XIX Amendment Installation*, Grand Central Station, Drenttel Doyle Partners)

VOICE OF SPECULATION, IMAGINATION, PERSONAL HISTORY, SCIENTIFIC CONVICTION . . . IT IS NOT THE SAME, SINGULAR VOICE OF AUTHORITY THAT SPOKE IN THE 19TH

CENTURY EXHIBIT. THE DEMANDS ON THE DESIGNER HAVE LIKEWISE CHANGED DRAMATICALLY. YET THOSE CHANGES HAVE ULTIMATELY MADE THE DESIGNER'S ROLE MORE

PROJECTS

The following inventory lists and describes the projects illuminating the typographical concerns of this book. Exhibition design firms from around the globe engage in an astounding array of topics and themes, creating environments for human experience and learning. The reader will find that many of these exhibitions are found in some of the most distinguished museums of the world; others are purely local and vernacular in scope. Within each of these settings, typography is fused with interpretive graphics, interactives, artifacts, and architectural structures, providing spaces that inform, entertain, satisfy curiosities, establish contexts and challenge the human intellect.

The projects presented in this chapter are also the subject of discussion in chapter 5, *A Closer Look.* The order of the projects remains consistent in both chapters for cross-referencing.

Altoona Railroaders Memorial Museum

Altoona, Pennsylvania, US

Christopher Chadbourne and Associates

American Airlines C.R. Smith Aviation Museum

Fort Worth, Texas, US

Zalisk Martin Associates

For Love of Days Gone By

Amsterdam,
The Netherlands

Marit van der Meer and Josephine Oudijn

Grasslands

National Zoological Park,
Washington, DC, US

Main Street Design, Inc.

The Railroaders Memorial Museum tells the stories of the workers who built, ran, and maintained the Pennsylvania Railroad. A two-story Broadway stageset, with a Hollywood scripted light and sound show, greets the visitor upon entry, while a full-scale, video-projected railroad call-boy confronts you upon entering the community area. Visitors become ghosted 1930s' railroaders in the bar-room mirror as they argue about joining the Union, go to work as an apprentice in the shop, ride a recreated K-4 locomotive, interactively experiment in the testing labs, learn railroad economics from a corporate CEO, and visit the 1939 World's Fair Railroad Pavilion. Bill Withuhn of the Smithsonian has termed it the finest museum of history in the United States, while the *Washington Post* has called it "a little boy's dream come to life."

The American Airlines C.R. Smith Aviation Museum is a new 19,000-square-foot museum focusing on the history of American Airlines and the science and experience of flight. Major exhibit areas include: the "History Wall" (with interactive and interpretive elements); *American Airlines in the Air* (interactive exhibits about how planes fly); *American Airlines on the Ground* (interactive exhibits about ground operations, navigation and communication); American Airlines *Maintaining the Fleet* (interactive exhibits about how aircraft/aircraft parts are tested, reviewed, repaired and reconstructed) and *Flightlab* (interactive exhibits about the science of flight).

What do a brush for mazzah crumbs, a money-box for de Joodsche blinde (a blind Jewish person) and a Johnny and Jones phonograph record have in common? They are all part of the Van Velzen collection of artifacts centered around Jewish life in The Netherlands. Recently, this collection was added to that of the Jewish Historical Museum in Amsterdam. The exhibition features a choice selection of artifacts from a vast collection of over four thousand items. Over a period of three decades, Van Velzen retrieved remnants from three centuries of Jewish life in The Netherlands. Things that appeared mundane and trivial were collected to offer an overall impression of what has long since disappeared.

Early in 1995 the National Zoo selected Main Street Design, Inc. to plan, develop and design a complete sequence of exhibit experiences and related interpretive elements for its new *Grasslands* habitat areas. This innovative and ambitious project is devoted to celebrating and exploring the North American Prairie. *Grasslands,* unlike most exhibits at the zoo, is not confined to a single site, but utilizes numerous relatively small individual pockets of new habitat and exhibits throughout the Zoo.

Hancock Park

**Interpretive Exhibit
for the La Brea Tar Pits**

Los Angeles, California, US

Sussman/Prejza & Co. Inc.

Hollandsche Schouwburg

Amsterdam,
The Netherlands

Victor Levie
and Monique Rietbroek

Kellogg's Cereal City USA

Battle Creek, Michigan,
US

Jack Rouse Associates

Liberty Science Center

Liberty State Park,
New Jersey, US

Donovan and Green,
a company of marchFIRST

Hancock Park is a unique urban setting situated along Wilshire Boulevard in the Miracle Mile section of Los Angeles. Home to both the Los Angeles County Museum of Art and the Page Museum of La Brea Discoveries, Hancock Park is a natural historic site where both science and art are combined in a public setting. The park, which contains natural tar pits and fossils, dates back to the Miocene and Pliocene eras when the Los Angeles basin was covered by sea. In 1913, G. Alan Hancock gave the 23-acre tract of land to the County of Los Angeles for the purposes of preserving and exhibiting its scientific features.

The Hollandsche Schouwburg was a small 19th-century theatre near the center of Amsterdam, at the edge of the Jewish neighborhood. During the German occupation, it served as a prison for Amsterdam Jews who were sent to concentration camps. Now it is a museum for children and memorial site. The "dark" side of the museum is a chronological story of the German occupation, which focuses on the societal rules the Germans enforced to arrange for the disappearance of the Jews from everyday life. As a result, their transportation to death camps occurred without too much protest. The "light" side reveals very personal stories about children smuggled from the Hollandsche Schouwburg, going underground and surviving. The memorial site contains the names of more than 100,000 Dutch Jews who were killed.

Kellogg's Cereal City USA is a 45,000-square-foot facility designed to entertain visitors while informing them of the impact the cereal industry and Kellogg's products have had on American culture – from nutritious breakfasts to Saturday morning cartoons. The center houses interactive exhibits, history timelines, richly themed theatres, immersive environments, an art gallery, a themed diner, shops and play areas. Jack Rouse Associates provided the overall creative thrust for Kellogg's Cereal City USA. Services included the design of all exhibits, theatres and interactive attractions; project management; research and writing; artifact selection; media production, and conceptual design of the unique building.

Donovan and Green's purpose was to help create a voice and identity befitting the overall tenor and educational philosophy for the new Liberty Science Center. This active, engaging, family- and child-centered 150,000-square-foot science center was conceived to reach a broad metropolitan audience from its New Jersey location. The communication strategy that evolved covered all areas of audience outreach and interaction within the institution. Component parts included a basic institutional identity, symbol design, environmental graphics and wayfinding system, marketing communication, fund raising, event and meeting solicitation, as well as sponsor-directed programs.

Look Hear, Art and Science of the Ear

The Welcome Centre for Medical Science, London, UK

Trickett & Webb Limited

The client's brief was to create an exhibition at the centre's new premises in London devoted to the art and science of the ear. Under the title *Look Hear*, the exhibition follows the path that sound takes through the ear. Through presentation of light and electron microscopic images, *Look Hear* enabled visitors to gain an increased understanding of the mechanisms of hearing. The exhibition also provided an opportunity for a group of artists from Bristol to explore the micro-architecture of the ear and present their discoveries to the public.

Odyssey

The Maritime Discovery Center, Seattle, Washington, US

West Office Exhibition Design

Odyssey is the centerpiece of the Port of Seattle's Bell Street Pier redevelopment. The museum provides an educational window on a busy international harbor and a dynamic maritime region. Through interactive exhibits and educational programs, visitors of all ages explore global marine trade, North Pacific fisheries, and Puget Sound's various maritime communities.

Philips Competence Centre

Eindhoven, The Netherlands

The Burdick Group

The challenge of this project was to present the total competency of this international corporation, with nine different product divisions, in one facility that would serve as their "front door" to visitors and business partners. The Centre is located in an existing circular and domed building, whose interior contains three exhibition levels or "rings," which were designed by The Burdick Group. After researching Philips product innovations, the Group determined that they all have grown from a set of shared "technical core competencies" – optics, motors, electronics, lighting, glass, materials and software. Interactive exhibits were developed to illustrate how each selected product innovation (i.e., Compact Disc (CD), High Definition TV (HDTV), compact lighting, medical products, etc.) was derived from the same set of "core competencies."

Possible Dreams

Popular Mechanics and America's Enthusiasm for Technology

Henry Ford Museum and Greenfield Village Dearborn, Michigan, US

Staples & Charles Ltd

The magazine *Popular Mechanics* has captured and reflected the "can do" spirit of the American character for over ninety years. Sponsored by Hearst Magazines and the Henry Ford Museum and Greenfield Village, this exhibition examines Americans' proclivity and fascination for transforming wild ideas into new technology and displays a wide range of original objects first seen in *Popular Mechanics*, from the winning 1902 electric race to early x-ray equipment.

Rock and Roll Hall of Fame and Museum

Cleveland, Ohio, US

The Burdick Group

Taxi Driver of the Year

Business Design Centre, London, UK

Trickett & Webb Limited

The 30th Anniversary Covers Tour

Rolling Stone Magazine

Traveling Exhibition

Pentagram

Urban Revisions

Current Projects for the Public Realm

Museum of Contemporary Art, Los Angeles, California, US

April Greiman Associates

The challenge of this project was to design a museum that informed and involved visitors with the subject matter, who – unlike visitors to other museums – already "own the art." The subject matter is presented in four perspectives: *The Historical Experience, The Social Experience, The Performers' Experience and The Visitors' (i.e. Fans) Experience.* To make the content come alive, The Burdick Group used the tools of Rock and Roll: sound, light, artifacts and memorabilia combined with dynamic exhibit forms and large scale imagery to create a new type of museum.

The *Taxi Driver of the Year* show is a fun day out for the family. The giant letters TAXI are displayed in an entertaining way, but they also function as carriers of serious messages for drivers considering joining Computer Cab's fleet. The graphic content demonstrates the benefits that the company offers its drivers and its success in gaining large corporate customers.

The traveling exhibition, *The 30th Anniversary Covers Tour,* is a celebration of the cover art and design of *Rolling Stone* magazine. Housed within a landscape dominated by the deconstructed letterforms used to form the name, *Rolling Stone*'s energetic and highly visual covers are reproduced and presented. As a traveling exhibit, the show was designed to be easily and quickly transported, assembled, and dismantled. Individual components were designed to function in a variety of spaces. The use of back-lit Plexiglas in panels and kiosks avoided potential lighting problems.

The exhibition *Urban Revisions: Current Projects for the Public Realm* was held at the Los Angeles Museum of Contemporary Art in 1994. It was curated by Elizabeth Smith, and the installation was designed by RoTo Architects. RoTo also helped to develop the content, as the exhibition featured architecture and other projects related to urban planning. April Greiman designed the exhibition's catalogue and theme panels, and suggested how they should be displayed as a seamless whole. The theme panels were two- and three-dimensional hybrids and were designed on the Macintosh computer. They contained photographic images, diagrams, and typography; but at the same time were what Greiman calls "ephemeral architecture" since the scale of the sheets of film measured 6 x 10 feet.

Village Works

Photographs by Women of China's Hunan Province

The Davis Museum, Wellseley, Massachusetts, US

Pentagram

Village Works: Photographs by Women in China's Hunan Province, exhibits photographs from a public health project in rural China. Photography provided an opportunity for a non-literate population from a remote area of the country to document their daily lives. The photographs communicated visually the reality of the lives of these people to individuals in power at the provincial level. The exhibit is designed to act as a bridge between the original documentary and social intent of the photographs and their value as an artistic statement. The intent, however, was not to present the photographs as fine art, but to retain their original intent.

World of Life

California Science Center, Los Angeles, California, US

West Office Exhibition Design

As one of four major theme areas of the California Science Center, the *World of Life* explores the life processes shared by all living things, from single-celled organisms to 100-trillion-celled human beings. The exhibit communicates to audiences of all ages and interest levels with its unique environments, hands-on exhibits and a children's *Discovery Room*. One highlight of the *World of Life* is a 15-minute production in the BodyWorks Theater, starring 50-foot long, anatomically correct "Tess," who demonstrates how the body maintains homeostasis.

Zum Schutz des Landes

Landeszeughaus Landesmuseum, Joanneum, Graz, Austria

Staples & Charles Ltd

Zum Schutz des Landes (In Defense of Styria) is a permanent introductory exhibition in the historic armory of the Austrian state of Styria. The exhibition introduces visitors to the armory and to the fabulous collection of arms and armor, explaining their significance, both symbolic and military. Together with Dr. Peter Krenn, Director of the Landeszeughaus, and project manager Thomas Köhler, Staples & Charles Ltd assembled and coordinated the diverse skills and talents available in Styria: fine steel working and cabinet-making, musicians, artists, sculptors and illustrators, giving the exhibition the magnificence of fine craftsmanship and artistic expressions.

A CLOSER LOOK

WINDOWS, MAPS, AND LABELS:
RETHINKING THE ROLE OF TYPOGRAPHY IN EXHIBITION DESIGN
ESSAY BY J. ABBOTT MILLER

AS A CHILD GROWING UP IN NEW YORK IN THE EARLY 1960S I USED TO RIDE THE MADISON AVENUE BUS TO SCHOOL AND THE THIRD AVENUE BUS HOME. LIKE MOST SMALL

Altoona Railroaders Memorial Museum

Altoona, Pennsylvania, US

Christopher Chadbourne and Associates

Client:
Railroaders
Memorial Museum
Project Director:
Christopher Chadbourne
Project Manager:
Antonio Treu
Senior Graphic Designer:
John Wrench
Project Size:
13,500 square feet
Project Budget:
$4,000,000

The logo of the Pennsylvania Railroad, which is used as a major design element on most graphic panels, sets up the typographic "look and feel" for the museum. This mark reflects the graphic and typographic character of the Age of Steam. Consequently, Copperplate was used as the signature font for all interpretive headlines. As this is a museum about people at work, the fonts also needed to convey a sense of strength. For this reason, a slab serif font, Serifa, was used as the second face in the type hierarchy. Its color, size, and placement give it instant recognition as important information, second only to the headline itself. Serifa represents quotes and subheads on the primary and secondary graphic panels and also the graphic rails. Being italicized sets it apart from the rest of the fonts and raises its visibility. Clarendon is third in the type hierarchy. Used as the body text typeface, it has low contrast for a serif font, giving it a high legibility factor for reversing out of black and a masculine/sturdy character.

1
Through visual and tactile means such as labeling typography, manual and computer-driven interactive devices, touch-screen interactive displays, motion-activated audio-video, and task simulators, the visitor revisits the 19th-century world of the railroad worker. This panel, which measures approximately 10 x 10 feet consists of rear-projected images, back-lit typography, an interactive graphic rail, and vitrines containing railroad artifacts.

2
One of five street signs identifying specific neighborhoods within the town of Altoona.

3
A graphic rail with legible, back-lit Serifa text revealing an oral history of Altoona neighborhoods. Red buttons are pushed to activate an audio version of the oral history and to reveal the location of the neighborhood on the map above the rail.

4, 5
These images illustrate the drama of the exhibition space, where visitors are immersed in an environment of light, sound, and images. Upon entering the museum, visitors are confronted by a full-size cast of a railroad call-boy created by Studio EIS.

ADVANCE OF HIGH-RISE DEVELOPMENT WAS ALREADY WELL UNDERWAY AND MY DAILY WALK TO THE BUS AND BACK USUALLY AFFORDED PLENTY OF OPPORTUNITIES TO

A graphic rail with descriptive text and images meanders through a convincing three-dimensional environment of railroad construction and workers.

7

This huge typographic panel sets the stage for a remarkable full-scale reconstruction of workers and locomotives. The large, centered, yellow Clarendon letters appear luminescent on a black background and within a red border.

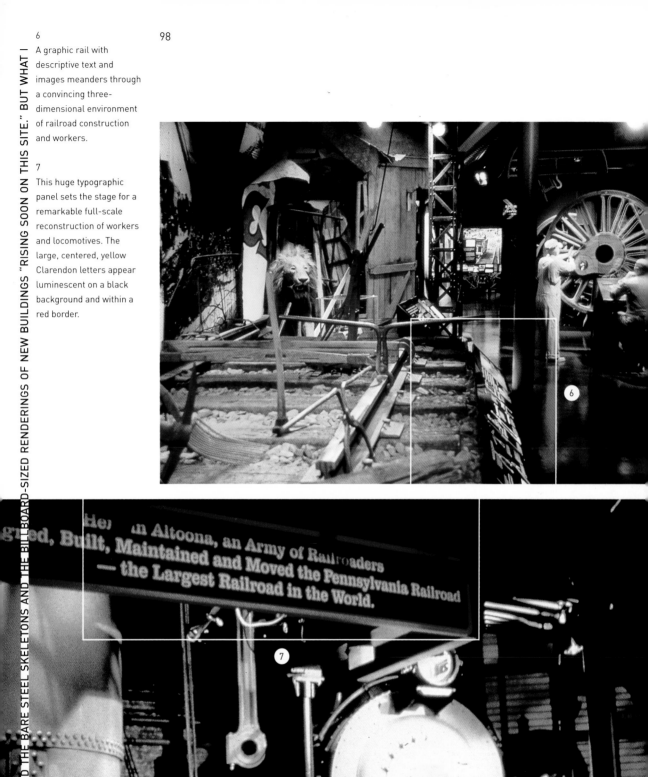

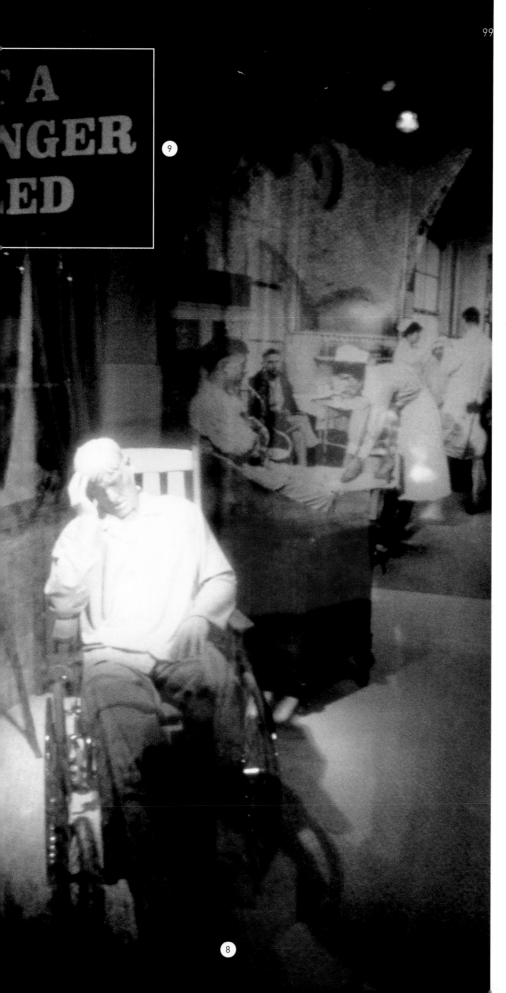

⑨

THE HEILER FAMILY... 1925
In Lancaster County, Pennsylvania, the great-grandfather of Dick Heiler was a professional butcher, providing meat for PRR commissary cars...

"My homestead was one block away from St. Mary's School where they taught German in the morning and English in the afternoon. My grandfather Harvey walked to work in the brass foundry and my daddy worked as a mechanic in the shops."

– Dick Heiler, Altoona Photographer

8
A ghostly portrayal of a hospital scene and a postman delivering a letter is achieved by means of rear-projected images onto a scrim. Through this transparent veil, one can also view a plaster cast of a man in a wheelchair and other objects from the period.

9
Impressive Clarendon type, reflecting the flavor of the period, is printed on the outside of the scrim. It boasts, "not a passenger killed."

10
Community signs with historic photographs and text housed within a typographic framework of rectilinear fields.

⑧

LIKED BEST WERE THE LITTLE WINDOWS CUT THROUGH CONSTRUCTION BARRICADES TO REVEAL WHAT WAS HAPPENING INSIDE. I'D STAND THERE AS LONG AS MY MOTHER

WHY IN THE WORLD ALTOONA?

Postcard, circa 1950, *DC Collection*

11

This primary graphic panel clearly reveals the expressed hierarchy of the typographic units: *1* the Copperplate headline, *2* the quote in Serifa, *3* body text in Clarendon. This hierarchical relationship is used throughout the exhibition to provide consistency. These assigned tasks of the typography make it easier for the visitor to negotiate and interpret information.

12

Copperplate headlines establish their position as the most dominant typographic element due to their larger size, appearance in all capital letters, and position at the top of the panels.

13

Notice the extreme line spacing of this quotation set in Serifa. This provides the panel with textural variety and color.

14

Clarendon is charged with the responsibility of presenting the body text. The type size, line length, and interline spacing insure the highest degree of readability. At the same time it presents information in a rugged tone, serving as a "voice" for the railroad workers of early twentieth-century Altoona.

"The valley of the Juniata offered advantages for a railroad line which were without rival."

– J. Edgar Thomson, Chief Engineer, 1848

Pittsburgh needed a rail connection to eastern ports, and the fledgling Pennsylvania Railroad competed fiercely with the already-established Baltimore & Ohio for the right to build it. The PRR eventually won, linking Pittsburgh with Philadelphia while mounting the Alleghenies in an almost impossible climb – at a spot in the wilderness chosen by Chief Engineer Thomson. Here, a base camp was established to support the enormous task.

The World's Largest Railroad City
The base camp was named Altoona, and it would become the world's largest railroad city. Trains were designed, built, tested, and repaired here. Its people would change the face of America and prove indispensable to its protection, from the Civil War to World War II.

WOULD LET ME, MY FACE GLUED TO THE FENCE. AT THE TIME THE CITY'S BUILDING TRADES WERE DOMINATED BY ONE BIG CONTRACTOR, THE GEORGE R. FULLER COMPANY,

GEOGRAPHY IS DESTINY

"We were the backbone of the railroad."

– Sam Pelligrino, PRR Machinist

From Harrisburg west, the Pennsylvania Railroad followed the riverbeds through the mountains to the foot of the Allegheny Plateau, Altoona was founded here, where – by 1854 – the PRR had climbed the east slope of the Ridge through engineering feats of world renown at Horseshoe Curve and Allegheny Tunnel at Gallitzin. Travel time to Pittsburgh was cut from 3½ days to 13 hours, and the west was formally opened to expansion. Altoona would ultimately support the infrastructure of the entire PRR system.

A Conveyor Belt to the World

If railroads were the streets of commerce of the industrial era, the Pennsy's Middle Division, with Altoona as its headquarters, was Main Street – a conveyor belt from America's heartland and the natural resources of the Allegheny Ridge, to eastern ports and back again.

15
A secondary exhibition panel which, though smaller in scale than the primary panel, remains true to the established typographical formula.

16
This example of a graphic rail is a variation on the exhibition's typographical syntax, demonstrating that unity and variety in typography can effectively coexist in the same space.

17
A street sign with Copperplate type revealing the name of the street. Appearing on the other side of the sign is a quote and images of the particular neighborhood.

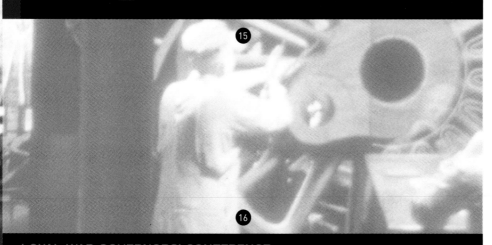

LOYAL WAR GOVERNORS' CONFERENCE

"A treasonable plot to abolish the Union, the Constitution and Negro slavery altogether."
– The New York Herald

"The second most decisive event of the Civil War."
– John Russell Young, Biographer

As Union fortunes reached a low point in late summer of 1862, a conference of Union governors was called to reaffirm loyalty to President Lincoln, his newly issued Emancipation Proclamation, and the war effort. Altoona – easily accessible by rail and boasting a luxury hotel – was the chosen site. In secret session, the governors pledged support to Lincoln and the Union.

The Advantages of Power
The Civil War marked a turning point for the PRR. Altoona became a strategic center for production of trains and transport of war materials and troops. Appointed Assistant Secretary of War, PRR Vice President Thomas A. Scott was said by some to have been slow to repair Confederate damage to the rival B&O Railroad's tracks, thus enhancing the importance and profits of his own employer.

LITTLE ITALY

WHOSE NAME ON BLUE AND WHITE SIGNS MARKED THE PERIMETERS OF THEIR PROJECTS. TO MY SIX OR SEVEN YEAR OLD EYES THAT SUGGESTED A PERFECTLY LOGICAL

American Airlines C.R. Smith Aviation Museum

Fort Worth, Texas, US

Zalisk Martin Associates

Client:
American Airlines
Project Manager:
Eileen Zalisk
**Exhibition Design
and Programming of
Interactive and
Interpretive Components:**
Zalisk Martin
Associates, Inc.
**Three-Dimensional
Design:**
Peter Martin
Antonio Treu
**Concept and Production
of the "History Wall":**
Mary McLaughlin, John
DeMao, John Malinoski,
Sandy Wheeler
Project Size:
19,000 square feet
(Museum); 120 linear feet
("History Wall")
Project Budget:
$4,000,000 +

This interactive and interpretive "History Wall" is divided into five segments representing five periods in the history of American Airlines (1918 – 29, 1930 – 39, 1940 – 59, 1960 – 18, 1979 – present). Each segment of the "History Wall" is made up of a series of display cases each constructed of 4 x 4 foot sheets of hanging Plexiglas. Here artifacts, photographs, newspaper articles and graphic elements combine with text to tell the story of American Airlines in each respective time period. The text and images are arranged to create a clear hierarchy of information and to communicate major content points with clarity. The artifacts and photographs seem to float or fly in the space creating an aesthetic quality which reinforces the exhibit content. The exhibit employs variations of Neue Helvetica, the corporate typeface of American Airlines, as it allowed for great flexibility and expressiveness.

1

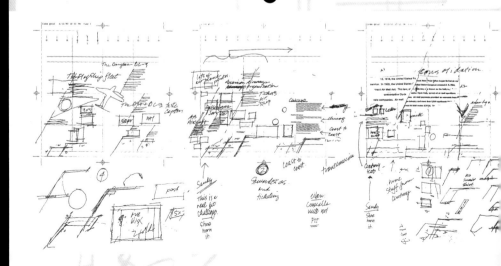

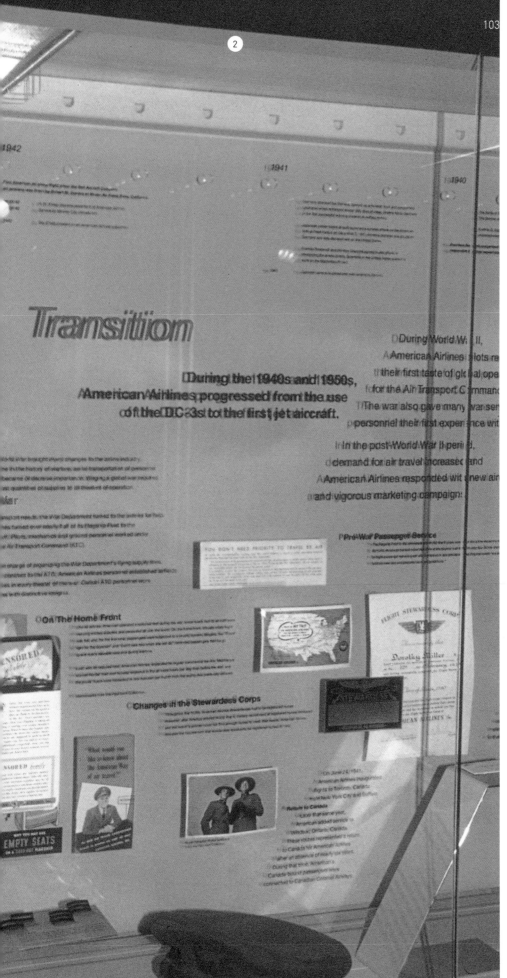

3

4

1
Layouts and notations for the "History Wall," a 120-foot linear presentation of text, objects, and artifacts.

2, 3, 4
The sense of motion and atmospheric quality of the "History Wall" is established by layering the 4 x 4-foot acrylic panels, using Neue Helvetica italic, and aligning specific text on a 60° angle. This angle is used in the design of the flags signifying the periods of American Airlines' history and the artifact display trays.

BUILD MORE!" ¶ IF THIS CONSTITUTED MY INITIAL EXPOSURE TO EXHIBITION TYPOGRAPHY, HOWEVER INADVERTENT, IT WAS ALSO MY FIRST ENCOUNTER WITH A

For Love of Days Gone By

Amsterdam,
The Netherlands

Marit van der Meer
and Josephine Oudijn

Client:
Jewish Historical Museum
Project Director:
Hetty Berg
Project Manager:
Bernadette van Woerkom
Senior Graphic Designer:
Marit van der Meer
Architect:
Josephine Oudijn

To emphasize the fact that all of the objects in the exhibition are items of common folk, the headings are all set in Courier, it being reminiscent of the typography of the typewriter, a common typeface available to everybody. The main text is set in Univers 55, a simple, clean typeface chosen for its ability to make exhibit information readable and accessible for the many visitors who are of an older age. The color red was used to highlight the favorite items of Mr. Van Velzen and also to articulate the different themes by which the objects were grouped in the space. The themes were used to bring an organized structure to the immense quantity of objects; they were not representative of the way the collection was originally assembled by Jaap Van Velzen.

1

Type is used in a very simple and understated way to counterbalance the enormous number of small items exhibited, and to project a quiet, unassuming voice.

2

The opening panel of the exhibition, which introduces the passionate and expansive collection of Jaap Van Velzen, is structured to present text in both Dutch and English. The treatment of the typography reflects the exhibit's subtitle, *Supreme Simplicity*.

De collectie Van Velzen
Liefdewerk oud papier
For the Love of Days Gone By
The Van Velzen Collection

In alle eenvoud
Supreme Simplicity

Wat hebben een matre-stoflertje, een collectebusje voor De Joodsche Blinde en een grammofoonplaat van Johnny and Jones met elkaar gemeen?
Ze maken alle deel uit van de waardevolle collectie Van Velzen over het Nederlandse joodse leven. Recent is deze verzameling aan de collectie van het Joods Historisch Museum toegevoegd. De tentoonstelling presenteert een eerste keuze uit het omvangrijke materiaal dat meer dan vierduizend stuks omvat.
'Verzamelen wat er niet meer was' stond Van Velzen voor ogen. In dertig jaar heeft hij ruim drie eeuwen joods leven in Nederland teruggehaald. Dingen die alledaags en betekenisloos leken, zijn bijeengebracht en geven samen een beeld van dat wat verdwenen is.

What do a brush for mazzah crumbs, a money-box for De Joodsche Blinde and a Johnny and Jones phonograph record have in common?
They all come from Van Velzen's valuable collection about Jewish life in the Netherlands.
Recently this collection was added to that of the Jewish Historical Museum. The exhibition features a choice selection from the vast material comprising over four thousand items.
Van Velzen aimed to 'collect what was no more'.
In three decades he retrieved over three centuries of Jewish life in the Netherlands. Things that appeared mundane and trivial are gathered to offer an overall impression of what has disappeared.

MYSELF SERVING AS THE PRINCIPAL OF AN EXHIBITION DESIGN FIRM, AND THAT EARLY INSIGHT INTO VISITOR BEHAVIOR IS AS ACCURATE AS EVER. THERE'S SIMPLY NO

Grasslands

National Zoological Park
Washington, DC, US

Main Street Design, Inc.

Client:
Smithsonian Institution
Project Director:
Melissa Gaulding
**Project Manager
and Exhibit Developer:**
J. Tevere MacFadyen
Exhibit Designers:
Michael Mercadante,
David Whitemyer
Graphic Designer:
Polly Baldwin
Project Size:
10 acres
Project Budget:
$700,000

In order to sustain a core interpretive message across distance, a series of conceptual signposts, or icons, are located at strategic points. These elements include specially designed kinetic sculptures, touchable globes showing the world's grasslands, and simple, strong introductory graphic images and text. All of the headline text is presented in Franklin Gothic, a tried and true work horse among typefaces that can always be counted on for clarity. Century Schoolbook was used for the body text. The typography is clean and understated and structurally related to imagery in exhibition panels by means of a versatile but carefully determined modular grid. Descriptive text, set flush left, ragged right appears in square or rectangular spatial units adjacent to colorful images to which it refers. The modular grid is the structural model for various exhibition components within the environment. Text most often appears in white, either reversed from photographs or solid background colors that complement colors in the photographs. The sizes of text are determined by a thoughtful consideration of visual hierarchy. Visitors encounter three distinct levels of interpretation. The first, an *Interpretive Center,* is housed in an open, barn-like shed structure, and features a high density of exhibitry, including hands-on opportunities, and multimedia components. The second, known

©Hoachlander – Davis Photography

©Hoachlander – Davis Photography

©Hoachlander – Davis Photography

1

Visual unity among the many components of the exhibit is established through a modular grid system of squares. This system is used as the basis for the proportions of panels and other related structures. By combining the smallest square unit into larger groups of rectilinear units, images and type are presented in many different sizes for visually dynamic displays. Panels in this exhibition are digital output embedded in fiberglass, and can withstand a variety of climates and weather conditions.

2

Headlines appear as lowercase Franklin Gothic Black. Text is Century Schoolbook set flush left, ragged right with generous interline spacing for optimum readability.

3

Support structures not only suggest blades of grass; they also embody a typographic character due to their simple geometry.

4

When done with care, skill, and attention to minute detail, optical adjustments in letter spacing allows legible type to be not only readable, but aesthetically pleasing as well.

5

A variation on the modular theme, this panel is fully saturated with a quilt of text and images.

JOB IS TO TAKE COMPLEX TOPICS AND RENDER THEM NOT ONLY UNDERSTANDABLE AND ACCESSIBLE BUT INTRIGUING, ENGAGING AND ENTERTAINING. OFTEN, WE PLAY A

6
Strategically placed signposts throughout the exhibit site link the various components of the exhibition together.

7
Simple lift-and-drop interactives add a kinetic dimension to the exhibit. They are used to pique the curiosity of visitors and engage them in the exhibit content.

8
Subheads and text are distinguished by both size and color.

9
This graphic panel, which integrates descriptive text and an interactive element, illustrates the hands-on emphasis of the exhibit.

as *Overlooks,* is presented within similar structures, but also focuses on direct interpretation of species and habitats on view, and incorporates fewer exhibit-based experiences than the *Interpretive Centers.* Finally, a new system of *Interpretive Rails* extends interpretation beyond the project's buildings and along visitor paths.

©Hoachlander – Davis Photography

10
A free-standing graphic panel offers yet another variation on the modular theme and a structure that adds three-dimensional variety to the exhibit.

11
For this floor panel, names and images of numerous organisms living in grasslands are combined into a complex and engaging relief.

ander – Davis Photography

ander – Davis Photography

ander – Davis Photography

©Hoachlander – Davis Photography

CONTENT IN ON THE SLY, LIKE A PILL TUCKED INTO A BIT OF HAMBURGER MEAT AND FED TO AN UNSUSPECTING DOG. AND MORE OFTEN THAN NOT, EVEN IN AN ERA OF

Hancock Park

**Interpretive Exhibit
for the La Brea Tar Pits**

Los Angeles, California, US

Sussman/Prejza & Co. Inc.

Client:
George C. Page Museum
of La Brea Discoveries
Project Director:
Paul Prejza
Project Manager:
Holly Hampton
Designer:
Niv Kasher
Project Size:
Seven interpretive exhibits
within a 23-acre site
Project Budget:
$85,000

①

The objective of this project was to enhance the social, as well as aesthetic value of Hancock Park as both a natural and cultural attraction. From the offset, the didactic nature of the exhibits implied the importance of the role which typography would play. Consideration in the selection of type styles was given to legibility, color and form, as well as compatibility with existing typographic systems for museums located at this site. The final result was a system that combined the sanserif font, Frutiger Roman with the serif font, Fenice.

Frutiger was the natural choice for the sanserif face. It not only provided legibility, but also helped to establish a visual link to the Los Angeles County Museum of Art, also being identified under the

②

④

Fossil Sites

Excavation Pit
Viewing Station 9

At this site, a great fissure-like vent filled with fossil bearing asphalt was excavated to a depth of 35 feet. The enclosed area represents only a small portion of the original excavation. The fossils included short faced bears, American lions, mastodons, sabertoothed cats, dire wolves, camels, horses and ground sloths. Over 10,000 fossils have been recovered from this site. The bones were associated with fossil wood, some of which has been dated at more than 40,000 years old.

Pit 9 is the main Rancho La Brea locality to yield Columbian mammoths. Remains of about thirty individuals were excavated and these ranged in age from newly born infants to elderly adults.

Pit 9 was excavated by the Los Angeles County Museum from November 18, 1913 to September 9, 1914.

Hancock Park

LACMA
Page
Museum
La Brea
Tar Pits

Park Hours: 6am-10pm

Page Museum

Restrooms

Lake Pit Walk

1
A symbol of the Gingko leaf is used for the logo of Hancock Park. This mark unifies various exhibit components.

2, 3
Directional signage, an important aspect of this outdoor exhibit environment is designed for ease of wayfinding. Because of its ability to be read easily at distances, Frutiger is the typeface used. The design fidelity of each individual character contributes greatly to clear typographic messages.

4
Note the unusual directional arrow that provides the signage with distinctiveness.

5
Porcelain enamel interpretive panels are located at the major excavation sites within the park. Photographs, diagrams, and typography are asymmetrically organized into dynamic and informative panels.

6
This locator sign identifies the Los Angeles County Museum of Art, the Page Museum, and the La Brea Tar Pits. The logotype and typographic units are sized and grouped for maximum clarity.

EXHIBITION TYPOGRAPHY IS LIKE BACKGROUND MUSIC. MOST PEOPLE NOTICE IT ONLY WHEN IT IS NOTICEABLY BAD. WHEN IT'S GOOD, TYPOGRAPHY CALLS LESS ATTENTION

7, 8

These interpretive panels reveal the compositional flexibility of the typographic system. While the treatment of the heads, text and captions, color, and organizational strategy remain constant, the panels appear uniquely different. For primary text, Fenice is set flush left, ragged right with generous interline spacing for ease of reading.

9

Parking signs are identified with a large capital letter *P* to distinguish them from other park signs.

10

This locator sign illustrates how maps and diagrams are designed with absolute simplicity and navigational clarity. The large numerals used to mark fossil site locations along the network of paths give visitors the confidence to freely explore the area.

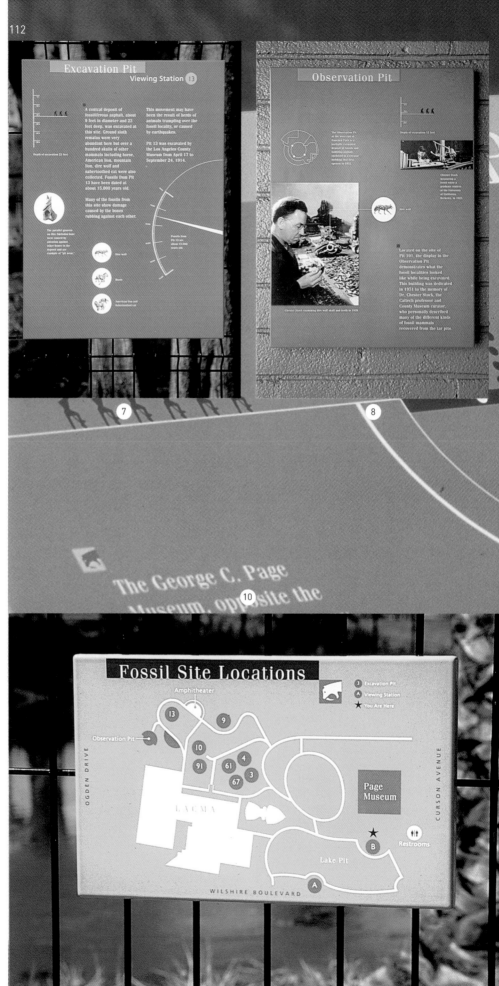

umbrella of Hancock Park. With this in mind the park itself needed an

identity that would work well when combined with the sanserif font.

To compliment the clean strokes of Frutiger, the modern, somewhat

condensed straight serif form of Fenice was chosen and developed in

combination with the Ginkgo leaf symbol as a vertical reading

logotype for the park. This sometimes controversial orientation

(because of legibility) helped to establish the hierarchy for

typographic messages within the program and Hancock Park as the

given "title." Fenice was used for the body copy of the exhibition

portion of the project as well. A 1/4 inch cap height with proper

leading allowed for ease of legibility at a comfortable viewing

distance.

11
The heights of graphic
panels and rails are
carefully determined to
satisfy the physical needs
of a wide-ranging
audience.

EXPERIENTIAL, WHETHER THE DESIGN AND TYPOGRAPHY ARE SIMPLE AND CONSERVATIVE OR UNCONVENTIONAL AND ABSTRACT, SUCCESSFUL TYPOGRAPHIC SOLUTIONS

114

The scientific interest in the tar pits lies within the written and visual history of the site. The porcelain enamel interpretive panels are located at the six major excavation sites within the park and identify the best view for each station. The content of the didactic panels combines typography, photography, and illustration. These elements are designed to visually display quantitative information including geologic time, animal life, and the preservation of the fossils excavated at Hancock Park. A major attraction for young and old alike, the researchers and designers gave every consideration to

12
The simplicity of this sign is rather deceptive, for the balanced placement of the type and image and the attention given to the harmonious spacing of the letters, words, and lines of type suggest an underlying complexity.

13
Exhibit components and signage are assigned different colors based on their given function. Orange is for supplementary information, yellow for directional information, and red for interpretive information.

ensure clear, concise communication. All elements, from the final

installed height of the panels, to the dynamics of color, typography

and composition, work together to signal the viewer from afar and

draw them in for a closer look.

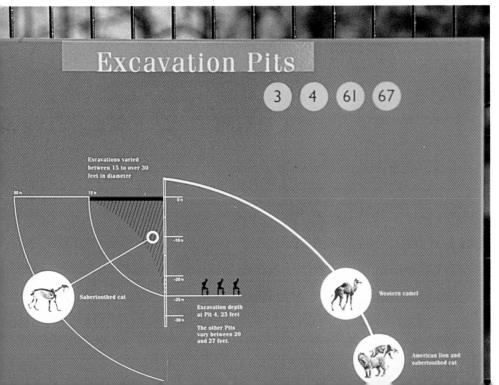

14
Typographic form and structure bring clarity to content. In this panel, it is clear that the large diagram is applicable to the 4 excavation sites specified by the numerals contained within circles.

15
Nothing in the Hancock Park exhibit system is left to chance. Differences in signage for womens' and mens' restrooms are established through variations in color, sign shape, figure, and plant icons.

MAKING THE BEST AND MOST SUCCESSFUL EXAMPLES OF INTERPRETIVE TYPOGRAPHY LESS MEMORABLE THAN THOSE THAT ARE TRULY TERRIBLE. ¶ SO WHAT DO WE AS

Hollandsche Schouwburg

Amsterdam,
The Netherlands

Victor Levie
and Monique Rietbroek

Client:
Hollandsche Schouwburg
Curator:
Judith Belinfante
Production Coordinator:
Bernadette van Woerkom
Senior Graphic Designer:
Victor Levie
Architect:
Monique Rietbroek

116

Because the museum possesses extremely powerful subject matter, there is no need for evocative typography. Factual information is presented in Univers 55 and 75. Information is brief, as many of the visitors are groups of school children on field trips. Informational details beyond interpretive panels are featured in a small brochure, which is sold to visitors. Personal quotations, appearing in Bodoni Italic, are stencilled onto the walls as a contrast to the facts.

Family names found at the memorial site are screened in white Univers 65 on 12 glass panels symbolizing the tribes of Israël. The panels are lighted at their sides and are mounted in 12 black alcoves. The thirteenth alcove, which is in the center, contains a plant symbolizing new life.

On the floor is an eternal flame surrounded by a short Psalm text in both Dutch and Hebrew. Also presented in Univers, these letterforms are cut from iron, and glued and set into the stone floor.

4

1
Start of the exhibition.
The story of the German
occupation is told in
chronological order.

2
The story of escape
and hiding (the "light side"
of the exhibition).

3
Overview of the "dark
side" of the exhibition.
A variety of techniques
are used to administer
type, including stencils,
transfers, and hand-
painted letters on walls
with rough surfaces.

4
In the memorial chapel,
all the last names of
Jewish families are silk-
screened on glass panels
and lit from the side. On
the blue wall, wooden
letters painted grey
reveal the story about the
disappearance of the
Jews. Psalm text in Dutch
and Hebrew is presented
in bronze-colored letters
set into stone flooring.

STRAIGHTFORWARD ENOUGH AND CORRESPONDS CLOSELY TO A SET OF COMMONLY ACCEPTED EXHIBITION DESIGN OBJECTIVES. FIRST, WE LOOK FOR NAVIGATIONAL CUES.

Kellogg's Cereal City USA

Battle Creek, Michigan, US

Jack Rouse Associates

Client:
Kellogg's Heritage
Foundation
Project Director:
Rob Morgan
Project Manager:
Ron Bunt
Project Size:
45,000 square feet (total
space); 27,000 square feet
(exhibits)
Project Budget:
$18,000,000

1
The welcoming arch leads
visitors into Cereal City's
town square.

2
The town square features
cobblestone streets and
whimsical facades which
lead into several exhibit
areas. The facades contain
an array of expressive
letterforms amidst many
cartoon-like shapes
and colors.

118

A panoply of typefaces based on those found on packaging and in cereal industry advertisements immerse the visitor into a world of color and fantasy. While the exhibition informs visitors of the enormous impact the cereal industry and Kellogg's products have had upon American culture, it is also a veritable study in American vernacular typography, with literally hundreds of period and ornamental typefaces represented in artifacts, reproductions, and

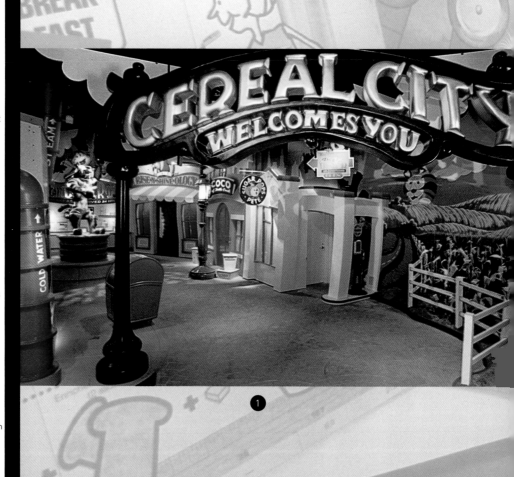

representations. Graphic panels, rails, history timelines, and interactives also feature typography in great variety. These include graphic panels with primary heads appearing in the typeface Atlas, section text in Futura Extra Bold, and the main body text in Futura Bold. Production line reader rails consist of the Machine Bold for primary heads, and Garamond for main body text.

3
A gigantic wall of cereal boxes configures the name *Kellogg's*.

4
Cereal box graphics and typography exude energy and playfulness. When greatly enlarged in scale, they engulf visitors into the world of make-believe.

5
Graphic rails with simple and clear typography stand in contrast to a profusion of artifacts from the famous Battle Creek Sanatorium, aiding in their interpretation.

6
Futura is used for this historical timeline. The readability of this typeface and the hierarchical manner in which it is presented makes the information very accessible.

7
This example reveals the characteristic visual energy of the exhibition and the integration of several exhibit devices, including artifacts, scroll-cut figures, and video.

ANOTHER – TO LAY DOWN A TRAIL OF CRACKED CORN. SECOND, WE LOOK FOR ORGANIZATIONAL CLUES. WE HOPE THE GRAPHICS WILL HELP US UNDERSTAND WHAT'S MOST

Liberty Science Center

Liberty State Park,
New Jersey, US

Donovan and Green,
a company of marchFIRST

Client:
Liberty Science Center
Project Director:
Nancye Green
Project Manager:
Adrian Levin
Clint Morgan
Project Size:
150,000 square feet

At Liberty Science Center's heart is a vast three-story atrium featuring hands-on and interactive exhibits for visitors of all ages. The architecture of the building suggests the mystery and discovery within its walls, having been described as "a cross between an art deco skyscraper and a nuclear reactor." Exhibits are designed around three basic themes: environment, health, and invention. In addition to coordinating all exhibit guidelines and standards, Donovan and Green developed the Center's visual identity program, environmental graphics, visual symbols, and wayfinding system. These important typographic components establish unity among a grand diversity of exhibits within the Center. The logotype is a marriage of type and image referring to the Center's location, and signifying the range of scientific exploration found at the Liberty Science Center – from solar systems to atoms. Helvetica Condensed is the typeface used for both the name of the center within the logotype and the greater wayfinding system within the building.

Exhibits
↓

©Wolfgang Hoyt, Photographer

©Wolfgang Hoyt, Photographer

1, 2
Within the Center's impressive atrium one sees elements of the distinctive wayfinding system. Yellow triangular banners draw attention to circular blue directional signs, providing not only a festive atmosphere, but also a consistent and rational wayfinding system. The scale of the highly readable Helvetica Condensed letters and positioning of the signs are carefully considered for ease of visitor navigation.

3
The logotype consists of two elements: the name of the Center and figurative letters signifying the location and content of the exhibits. The outreaching arm reminds us that Liberty Science Center is in the shadow of the Statue of Liberty and also conveys a sense of freedom of exploration and scientific investigation. The graphic planetary orbit and the formula for energy both utilize features of the letterforms: the counter-form of the S is one of the orbiting planets, and the C is part of the formula.

WHAT WE NEED TO KNOW, AND IDEALLY, THOUGH RARELY, JUST THAT: NO MORE AND NO LESS. ¶ ANSWERING THE SECOND QUESTION IS MORE DIFFICULT, BECAUSE IT

Look Hear, Art and Science of the Ear

The Wellcome Centre
for Medical Science,
London, UK

Trickett & Webb Limited

Client:
The Wellcome Trust
Project Director:
Terry Trickett

The primary display technique for this exhibition is the use of three-dimensional, wall-mounted cases. These cases contain three distinct layers of information. The background layer consists of images generated from both light and electron microscopes. The abstract and relatively simple appearance of these micro images enables them to function as backdrops to the two outermost layers of information. The middle layer consists of interpretive artworks by Bristol artists responding creatively to the micro-architecture of the ear. The front layer is a curved, clear acrylic panel with text and diagrams explaining the hearing process. The acrylic panels also serve to protect the art.

Gill Bold, a simple but expressive sanserif typeface, was selected for its excellent legibility, and for its ability to be cut from self-adhesive film and affixed to the surface of the curved Plexiglas panels. This type, which once applied appears to "float" in space above the art objects, was reproduced in a warm buff color. Special lighting emphasizes the floating type and helps retain its visibility.

Photograph ©Ian McKinnell

Photograph ©Ian McKinnell

Photograph ©Ian McKinnell

1
This overview reveals the main components of the exhibition: wall-mounted, three-dimensional display cases; a free-standing entrance panel announcing the exhibit; and a low display platform featuring a three-dimensional model of the ear.

2
The free-standing display panel announcing the exhibit is similar in structure to the display cases, but also contains a video monitor that presents three educational videos on the subject of hearing.

3
The floor display platform with a detailed model of the ear's anatomy.

4
The typography on the display cases is 9mm high. It is sophisticated and refined, both in terms of formal articulation and color.

EXHIBITION CAN COME AWAY WITH COMPLETELY DIFFERENT IDEAS ABOUT WHAT IT WAS ABOUT. SOME PEOPLE LIKE RULES AND BOUNDARIES. THEY WELCOME THE

5

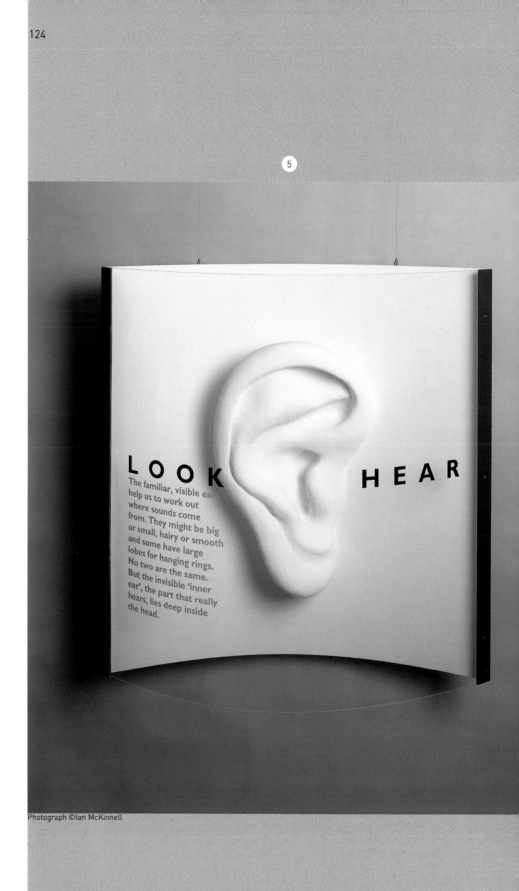

LOOK **HEAR**

The familiar, visible ear help us to work out where sounds come from. They might be big or small, hairy or smooth and some have large lobes for hanging rings. No two are the same. But the invisible 'inner ear', the part that really hears, lies deep inside the head.

Photograph ©Ian McKinnell

6

This is one of the two rows of hairs on a detector that sends signals to the brain.

Photograph ©Ian McKinnell

5
The title display case is representative of the fusion of typography, images, and three-dimensional objects into elegant, transparent constructions.

6
This sample display case reveals the visual complexity that is possible with the use of three-dimensional objects and the resulting interplay of light and shadow.

THE TEXTS. ¶ SOME TAKE THE OPPOSITE TACK. THEY PAY NO ATTENTION AT ALL TO THE INFORMATION THAT'S PROVIDED FOR THEM AND RELY INSTEAD ON WHAT THEY

Odyssey

The Maritime
Discovery Center
Seattle, Washington, US

West Office
Exhibition Design

Client:
Odyssey, The Maritime
Discovery Center
Exhibition Design:
West Office
Exhibition Design
Graphic Designers:
Henrike Aengenendt
Alexandra Donlon Treene
Rachel Hinman
Diane Marsens
Megan Simpson
Illustrations:
Tony Morse
Project Size:
30,000 square feet
Project Budget:
$5,000,000

Odyssey, The Maritime Discovery Center is an exciting educational resource and visitor attraction located on the Seattle waterfront at Bell Street Pier. Offering a spectacular view of Elliott Bay and the marine surroundings, it celebrates the Northwest's maritime character, providing a unique place to discover the maritime community's contemporary influence. *Odyssey*'s three main galleries feature more than 40 state-of-the-art, high-tech exhibits, which through hands-on and interactive demonstrations, visitors are able to discover the secrets of a working waterfront, the basics of nautical operations, and the latest in commercial fishing technology. Typography throughout this multi-faceted exhibition is simple and clean, but also well-suited in character and aesthetic to the content. Primary typefaces include Akzidenz Grotesk Bold for heads, Regular for captions, and Matrix for text. Garamond Semibold is used for secondary applications.

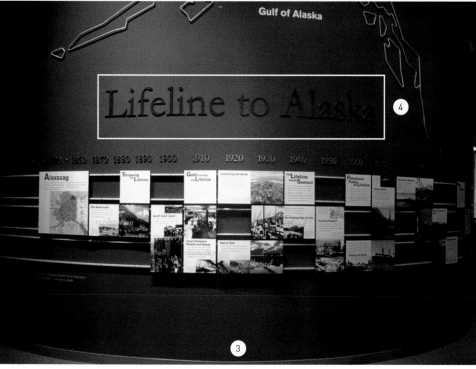

1
This welcoming interactive enables visitors to explore the diverse aspects of the Puget Sound by pressing specified buttons.

2
The opening screen of the interactive reveals an active and inviting layering of Akzidenz Grotesk and Garamond Italic.

3
A modular system of square graphic panels provides a clear and versatile structure for this timeline.

4
Three-dimensional Garamond letters are surface-mounted to achieve hierarchical prominence in the timeline. Letter and word spacing achieved with careful optical adjustment – as shown here – is a critical production requirement.

EXTERNAL PRESSURE. THEY'RE SWAYED BY THE PREVAILING MOOD OF THE GROUP VISITING WITH, OR THEY'RE SIMPLY INTIMIDATED BY THE EXPERIENCE OF BEING IN A

5

The *Wild Salmon* exhibit is an exemplary example of blending parts into a harmonious yet complex whole, and the integration of typography as a seamless unifier of these parts.

6

The subtle shift in the size and angle of the words *Wild* and *Salmon* provides the title with visual distinction and memorability. Also, the asymmetry of the heads in the graphic panels bring an element of informality to the exhibit.

7

Large-scale typography, extending the length of a montage of giant photographs, thematically unifies the images.

8

Typography not only identifies, it also sets the stage for a replica of the Purse Seiner, a fishing vessel of the Puget Sound. A flip-book located at the base of the model is consistent in typographic treatment with the exhibition.

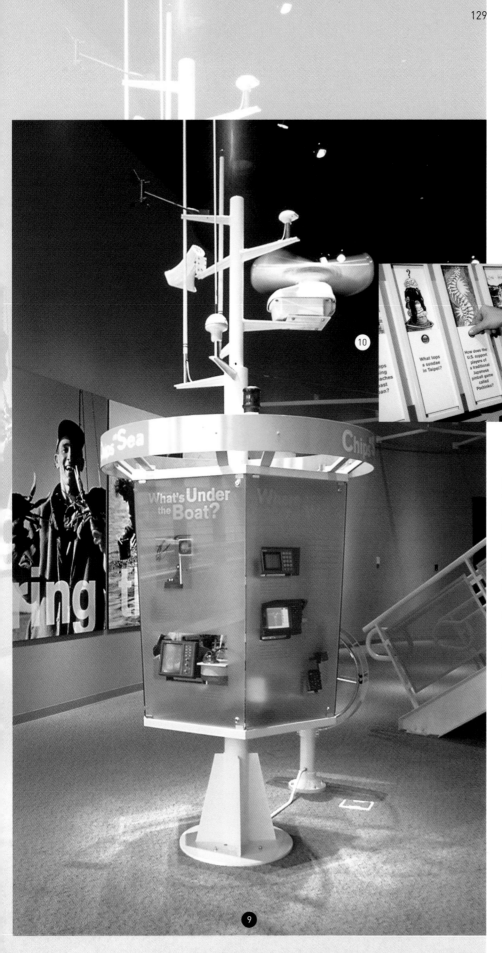

9
The *Ships at Sea* exhibition features an interactive kiosk that resembles an actual ship. Typography is integrated naturally into the components of the structure.

10
Lines of Akzidenz Grotesk type ask questions and encourage visitors to push interactive buttons on this side panel for answers.

AND SON APPROACH AN ANIMAL ENCLOSURE. THE SON RAN AHEAD, AS SONS DO, AND DAD HAD TO HURRY TO CATCH UP. HE ARRIVED AT THE RAIL SLIGHTLY OUT OF BREATH.

Philips
Competence
Centre

Eindhoven,
The Netherlands

The Burdick Group

Client:
Philips, The Netherlands
Project Directors:
Bruce Burdick
Susan Burdick
Project Manager:
Bruce Lightbody
Graphics Director:
Cindy Steinberg
Project Size:
40,000 square feet

A circular competency diagram was developed which became the "road map" to all of the exhibits, as well as the main menu access to the interactive computer programs that were developed as part of the exhibition. Located on each graphic panel, the highlighted part of the diagram indicated which of the technical core competencies contributed to the particular innovation demonstrated. For example, the development of the Compact Disc utilized all core competencies, while Compact Fluorescent Lighting utilized only five of the total set of eight.

The written copy for the exhibit is organized within a hierarchy of information: area title, headline, subtitle and text. Most of the interactive exhibits are organized on exhibit "armatures," a modular exhibit support system. The area title for each product innovation is located on the central glass panel of the armature, while each exhibit graphic panel contains the headline, subtitle, and text with the competency diagram.

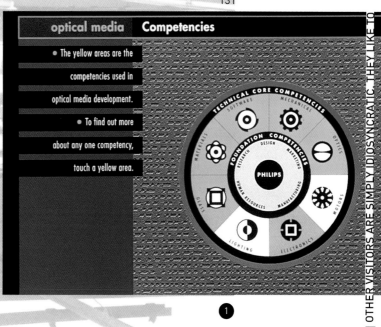

optical media   Competencies

- The yellow areas are the competencies used in optical media development.
- To find out more about any one competency, touch a yellow area.

1
The competency diagram as displayed on a computer touch screen.

2
Interactive exhibits designed to display a car navigation (CARIN) system, utilizing both vertical graphics and floor graphics. The floor graphics are linked and activated by the computer program which appears on screens on vertical panels.

3
Exhibits use a combination of written documentation, graphics, diagrams, and interactive displays to describe the specific innovation and the competencies that aided in the exhibit's development.

4
This foundation competency exhibit "wall" consists of vertical modular elements which combine LCD monitors, graphics, and artifacts to illustrate the company's competencies in market-ing, design, research and development.

SAID SO PLAIN AS DAY. BUT HE WASN'T LOOKING AT THE GRAPHICS; HE WAS TRYING TO KEEP UP WITH HIS SON. ¶ OTHER VISITORS ARE SIMPLY IDIOSYNCRATIC. THEY LIKE TO

Possible Dreams

Popular Mechanics and America's Enthusiasm for Technology

Henry Ford Museum and Greenfield Village, Dearborn, Michigan, US

Staples & Charles Ltd

Client:
Henry Ford Museum and Greenfield Village
Project Director:
Dr. Harold K. Skramstad
Project Manager:
Mary Seelhorst
Total Design:
Staples & Charles Ltd
Graphic Designer:
Ramona Ryabik Carter
Three-Dimensional Design:
Robert Staples
Philip Brady
Project Size:
5,000 square feet
Project Budget:
$250,000

The type and graphic styles of this temporary exhibition reflect the mood of the magazine: direct, functional, resourceful, and often unexpectedly, seemingly unintentionally, humorous. Headlines, dates, and question marks, set in Permanent Massive, are strong and direct. The sub-headlines and interpretive texts, in variations of Univers, are informational and functional. Quotations, all from *Popular Mechanics*, are set in Univers 67 Oblique.

From the first issue at the turn of the century, *Popular Mechanics* has had an editorial style that presents new discoveries, fascinating facts and bits of information, and encourages readers to make useful things from available parts. In this spirit, the exhibition uses billiard balls as object numbers, bowling balls for the footings of text panels made from hollow-core doors, and common metal extrusions and cardboard "sona" tubes, normally used for casting cement pylons, as construction and support elements.

Constructed in 1992, before multi-colored digital outputs were affordable or even available, all of the graphics – with the exception of large cut-out letters – are oversized xerox outputs; some are hand-colored, and all are produced on equipment normally used for

large architectural drawings.

1
Counterpoints are achieved in this space through rectilinear graphic panels, typefaces, and the contrasting dissonant troupe of oblique panels and objects.

2
Geometric counterforms of the typeface Permanent Massive create rhythmic lines in the large-scale panels. The typeface works unusually well with Univers 67, also a sanserif typeface, as it achieves a contrasting distinctiveness through its sturdiness and presentation in all caps.

3
Large cut-out letters, graphic panels, and innovative hanging objects carry on a lively dialogue of angle and asymmetry. These constructions are reminiscent of El Lissitzky's *Prouns*.

TO BE DIFFICULT, THEY SIMPLY HAVE A DIFFERENT WAY OF UNDERSTANDING THEIR WORLD. LIKE CHILDREN, THEY CONSTRUCT THEIR OWN LOGICAL FRAMEWORKS. ANOTHER

4

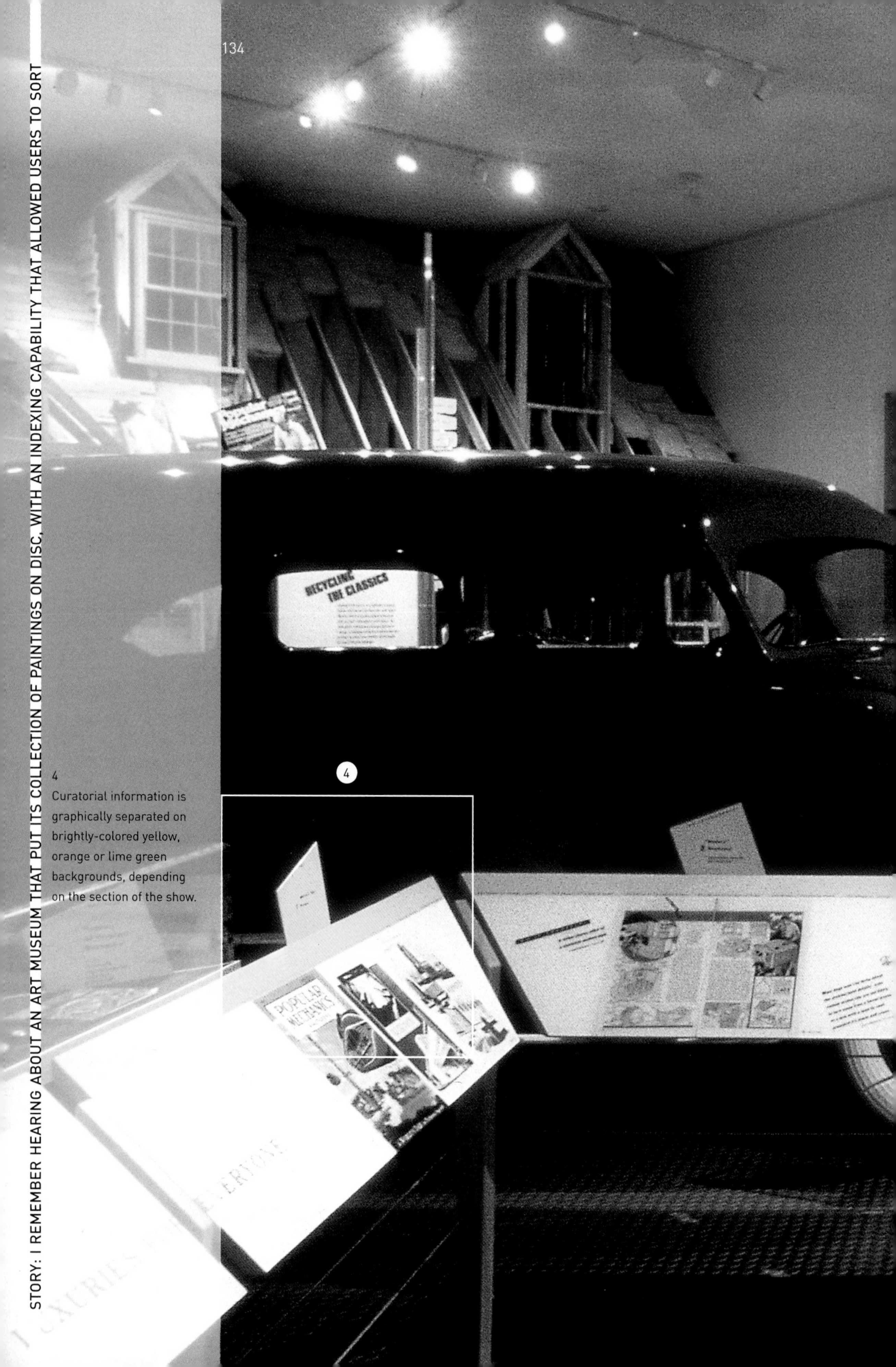

4
Curatorial information is
graphically separated on
brightly-colored yellow,
orange or lime green
backgrounds, depending
on the section of the show.

5
The reader rails which
also serve as protective
barriers hold whimsical
assemblages of images,
articles and quotations
from *Popular Mechanics*.

5

THE CONTENTS ANY WAY THEY CHOSE. WHAT THEY DISCOVERED WAS THAT THE FORMAL ACADEMIC CATEGORIES FAVORED BY ART HISTORIANS WEREN'T USED MUCH BY

Rock and Roll Hall of Fame and Museum

Cleveland, Ohio, US

The Burdick Group

Client:
Rock and Roll Hall of
Fame and Museum Board
Project Directors:
Bruce Burdick
Susan Burdick
Project Manager:
Bruce Lightbody
Graphics Director:
Stuart McKee
Project Size:
35,000 square feet

The graphic design of this exhibition incorporates a combination of traits that are significant to the interpretation of Rock and Roll. The visual system allows for a wide range of compositional variation by employing a typographic grid that accommodates a diverse range of text and solutions. Graphics range from those that are visually spare to dense, some with graphic images, and some with text only. The resulting versatility maintains stimulation among the museum's visitors as they encounter the range of solutions, and ensures a striking assortment of panels regardless of a particular exhibit's requirements.

An essential requirement of the exhibit graphics is that they maintain as timeless a visual presence as possible. The designers therefore avoided the use of period idiosyncrasies as primary design elements, but the system allows for the incorporation of details that reflect the sensibilities of various eras, where appropriate.

1
Text, graphics, artifacts, and audio reveal the creative processes leading to the songs selected for the exhibit.

2
Vertical "time markers" identify the various time periods of Rock and Roll. The accompanying text describes the periods in detail. Serving as the primary typeface, Franklin Gothic is expressed in abundant variation from exhibit to exhibit. Here, the vertical, slightly overlapping configuration of the dates reveal this visual diversity.

3
For the *One Hit Wonders* exhibit, typography plays a pivotal role in the establishment of a totally integrated exhibit environment. Text stretches dramatically along a curved wall to achieve a textural resonance, while song titles, artist's names, and descriptive text are functionally structured for maximum interpretive clarity.

GIRLS FAVORED IMAGES WITH DOGS OR HORSES. LITTLE BOYS LIKED BATTLES. ¶ WHICH BRINGS ME TO THE MATTER OF AUDIENCE, THE PEOPLE FOR WHOM WE OSTENSIBLY

DO WHAT WE DO. EXHIBITION DEVELOPERS AND DESIGNERS SPEND A LOT OF TIME THINKING ABOUT VISITORS, TRYING TO UNDERSTAND WHO THEY ARE AND WHAT THEY

4
For the exhibit, *Don't Knock the Rock*, a layering of typography, large-scale photography, and video dazzles the visitor.

4

WANT AND HOW BEST TO REACH THEM. BUT IT SOMETIMES SEEMS THAT WE SPEND ALMOST AS MUCH TIME COMPLAINING ABOUT OUR AUDIENCES (OR, ALTERNATIVELY, OUR

Taxi Driver of the Year

Business Design Centre,
London, UK

Trickett & Webb Limited

Client:
Computer Cab
Project Director:
Terry Trickett

CLIENTS), LAMENTING THEIR LACK OF CURIOSITY AND THEIR RELUCTANCE TO TAKE RISKS. AND LURKING SOMEWHERE DEEP INSIDE US IS THE SENTIMENT, SELDOM

Unquestionably, the dominating visual elements of this exhibit are the monumental letterforms composing the word "TAXI." These letterforms do more, however, than announce the content of the exhibition. They define the territory of the exhibit and establish firm control of its boundaries, creating a robust yet uninhibiting presence in a larger space that would dwarf a less exuberant presentation.

The huge three-dimensional letterforms were designed as free-standing platforms that contain text, graphics, illustrations and maps. Information on the planar sides of the letterforms provides details about the company for those who might be considering joining its fleet. The whimsical dot floating above the "i" references the satellite positioning system used by the Computer Cab company.

1
The typography incorporated in the graphic panels of the free-standing letterforms informs the public of the company's different cab liveries and promotes their services.

2
The satellite – perceived also as the dot of the "i" – is suspended high above the floor. In the immense space of the building, it can be seen from a distance, marking the location of the exhibit.

3
The giant letters, 3.5 meters or approximately 11 1/2 feet high, aid in defining the space and give a sense of order to the exhibition.

4
The primary typeface for text is Univers 55, supported by a collection of other display faces. The graphic and informational content describes benefits offered by the company as well as the success it has had in increasing its customer base to include large corporate clients.

EXPRESSED, THAT IF ONLY OUR CLIENTS AND VISITORS WERE AS HIP AND SMART AS WE WERE WE COULD DESIGN MUCH BETTER EXHIBITIONS. ¶ THIS ARROGANT NOTION IS

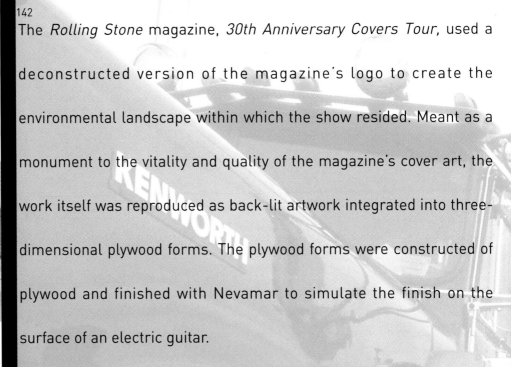

The 30th Anniversary Covers Tour

Rolling Stone Magazine

Traveling Exhibition

Pentagram

Client:
Rolling Stone magazine
Project Director:
J. Abbott Miller
Project Manager:
Jane Rosch
Designers:
J. Abbott Miller
James Hicks
Paul Carlos
Scott Devendorf
Project Size:
3,000 square feet

The *Rolling Stone* magazine, *30th Anniversary Covers Tour,* used a deconstructed version of the magazine's logo to create the environmental landscape within which the show resided. Meant as a monument to the vitality and quality of the magazine's cover art, the work itself was reproduced as back-lit artwork integrated into three-dimensional plywood forms. The plywood forms were constructed of plywood and finished with Nevamar to simulate the finish on the surface of an electric guitar.

1

The typography and typographic forms, created as an extension of the *Rolling Stone* typographic voice, were also meant to be central to the formal language of the three-dimensional environment. The strength of the large typographic forms was essential to branding the environment with the company persona. This allowed the exhibit to appropriate the varied spaces in which it was to appear.

1
The type for the large free-standing structures was derived from the logo and masthead of *Rolling Stone* magazine.

2
Back-lit Plexiglas panels and large-scale letter-forms interact to create an environment that is primarily defined by the formal language of typographic elements.

3
The highly dimensional and deconstructed letter-forms become sculptural elements that occupy and order the space. Because of their scale in relation to the visitor, they direct and structure the viewer's experience.

©Geri Bauer Photographics, Inc.

©Geri Bauer Photographics, Inc.

IN EXHIBITION DESIGN. TRADITIONALLY, TYPOGRAPHY HAS ALWAYS PLAYED THE STRAIGHT MAN IN EXHIBITION DESIGN. WHILE BELLS AND WHISTLES AND DRAMATIC

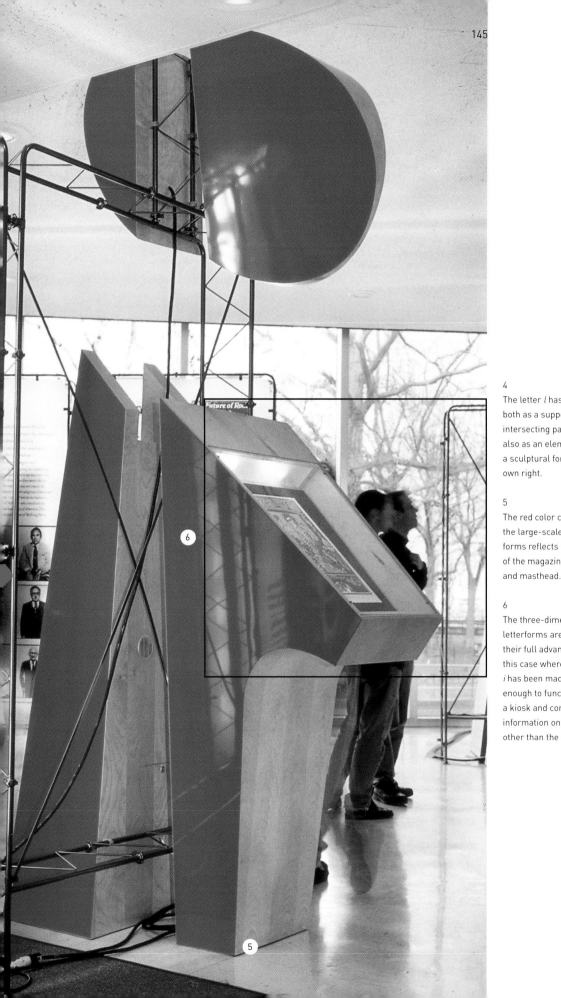

4
The letter *l* has been used both as a support for intersecting panels and also as an element that is a sculptural form in its own right.

5
The red color chosen for the large-scale letter-forms reflects the color of the magazine's logo and masthead.

6
The three-dimensional letterforms are used to their full advantage, as in this case where the letter *i* has been made wide enough to function as a kiosk and contain information on a plane other than the vertical.

LIGHTING EFFECTS SWIRL AROUND THE HEADS OF DELIGHTED OR BEWILDERED VISITORS, TYPOGRAPHY HAS ALWAYS PROVIDED A RELIABLE PATCH OF SOLID GROUND. TO

Urban Revisions

Current Projects for the Public Realm

Museum of
Contemporary Art,
Los Angeles, California, US

April Greiman Associates

Client:
Museum of
Contemporary Art,
Los Angeles
Project Director:
Elizabeth Smith
Project Managers:
April Greiman
Michael Rotondi,
RoTo Architects

The exhibition *Urban Revisions: Current Projects for the Public Realm* was held at the Los Angeles Museum of Contemporary Art in 1994. It was curated by Elizabeth Smith and the installation was designed by RoTo Architects. RoTo also contributed to content development, as the exhibition featured architecture and other projects relating to urban planning. Greimanski Labs designed the exhibition catalog and the theme panels, and suggested how the panels should be presented as a seamless whole. The panels are what Greiman refers to as "ephemeral architecture," a term to describe the large hybrid structures as having both two- and three-dimensional aspects. They were produced on sheets of transparent film measuring 6 x 10 feet and designed on the Macintosh computer. Visitors are able to see through the film, beyond photographic images, diagrams, and typography to people moving around the exhibition beyond, not unlike the visual phenomenon in an actual urban environment. These textural panels are skillfully integrated with other graphic panels and exhibit components. The primary typeface used in the panels was OCR-A.

1

Urban Revisions explores a wide range of fresh, responsive, and provocative approaches to the revisioning of cities by some of today's most creative and engaged architects, urban planners, and citizens.

2

The transparent theme panels ("ephemeral architecture") provide a medium that conceptually includes visitors as part of the exhibit.

3

The *New Neighborhood* theme panel reveals a highly textured use of the typeface OCR-A in combination with dense fields of images to metaphorically suggest the complexity of the urban fabric.

4

The *Wall of Graffiti* presents striking images of "urban artworks," accompanied by white OCR-A text in black rectilinear fields that reflect the visual vocabulary of the theme panels.

ALSO BEEN TRUE BECAUSE UNTIL QUITE RECENTLY IT WAS TOO DIFFICULT AND EXPENSIVE TO MAKE TYPOGRAPHY BE ANYTHING ELSE. TODAY TYPE CAN DO JUST ABOUT

Village Works

Photographs by Women of China's Hunan Province

The Davis Museum
Wellsley, Massachusetts, US

Pentagram

Client:
Davis Museum and Cultural Center
Project Director:
J. Abbott Miller
Designers:
J. Abbott Miller
James Hicks
Jeremy Hoffman
Project Size:
2,500 square feet

The primary concern was how to best present photographs of a documentary and anthropological nature within the context of an art museum. The photographs were digitally output on paper and silk and then stretched and hung on kiosks constructed of plywood and steel. The design of the kiosks, taken from Chinese characters, and readable from certain angles, were placed to suggest a village center or marketplace. The forms of Chinese characters play a major role in helping to create the cultural context.

The text was presented bilingually and Scala Sans was chosen for the English version because of its clean and open characters that echoed the qualities of Chinese characters. The largest text, on the rear wall, is a well known Maoism that states, "women are half the sky."

1
The text is treated bilingually, in Chinese and English, and recessively so as not to compete with the photographs.

2
English text is set in Scala Sans with an interline spacing that aids readability. Text units and photographs are asymmetrically balanced within modular spaces creating visual activity and a degree of informality.

©Geri Bauer Photographics, Inc.

©Geri Bauer Photographics, Inc.

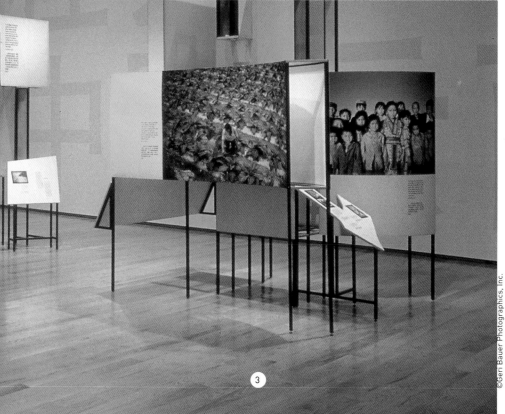

©Geri Bauer Photographics, Inc.

©Geri Bauer Photographics, Inc.

4

3
The subtle but monumental background text links with the forms of the pavilions and helps to establish an overall context.

4
From certain angles the kiosks read as specific Chinese characters. The central kiosk forms the character for "woman."

TYPOGRAPHY OF ITS TRADITIONAL INFORMATIONAL ROLE AND TURN IT LOOSE TO SHAPE THE LARGER VISITOR EXPERIENCE. ¶ WHEN THAT HAPPENS – AND IT HAS ALREADY

World of Life

California Science Center
Los Angeles, California, US

West Office
Exhibition Design

Client:
California Science Center
Exhibition Design:
West Office
Exhibition Design
Graphic Designers:
Alexandra Donlon Treene
Henrike Aengenendt
Megan Simpson
Illustrations:
Rick Jones
Project Size:
20,000 square feet
Project Budget:
$4,200,000

The typographical challenge of the *World of Life* exhibition was to increase visitor comprehension and understanding of the fact that all living things (from the single-celled bacterium to the 100 trillion-celled human being) share common life processes. Through unique environments such as the 55-foot-long *Life Tunnel*, hands-on exhibits, and a children's *Discovery Room*, typography aids in revealing life mysteries to a wide audience. Within the main exhibit hall, five galleries feature the five processes of creating, controlling, supplying, energizing, and defending life. To bring organizational and hierarchical clarity to the space, each of these content areas was visually and structurally zoned by means of large, circular canopies suspended from the ceiling. Lining these structures are the individual gallery names appearing as large cut-out metal letters. These area names appear in Gill Sans, which is also the typeface used for heads and captions throughout the exhibition. Body text is set in Garamond Semibold.

Cells Coming Together

2

3

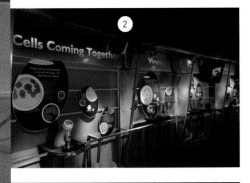

4

5

6

1
The *Supply Network* exhibit is identified by a circular canopy to which its name in large cut-out metal letters is pin-mounted. This typography, along with all other Gill Sans elements appears in dark purple. Garamond text appears consistently in cool gray. Mirroring the canopy, on the floor, is a circular carpet in the color assigned to the area (each is assigned a different color to further establish identity and separation).

2, 3
The *Cell Lab* immerses visitors into the repro-duction and life of cells through hands-on displays, models, and circular interpretive panels reminiscent of cells.

4
The 55-foot *Life Tunnel* introduces visitors to the *World of Life*'s educational message: "from apple trees to honey bees, we're more alike than you think." This is accomplished with rear-illuminated photo-graphy and reflective rails containing short facts about the interconnect-edness of all living things. These statements are set poetically in Gill Sans Bold.

5, 6
Two views of a hands-on interactive about cock-roaches reveals the participatory nature of the exhibits. The graphic rail in front and panel in the back reveal the simplicity and clarity of the typographic information.

WILL WE NO LONGER NEED THE FAMILIAR COMFORTS OF CONVENTIONAL TYPOGRAPHY TO GUIDE AND INFORM US ALONG THE WAY? WILL WE CLING TO TRADITIONAL TYPE

Zum Schutz des Landes

Landeszeughaus
Landesmuseum,
Joanneum, Graz, Austria

Staples & Charles Ltd

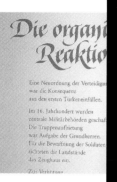

Client:
Landesmuseum
Joanneum
Project Director:
Dr. Peter Krenn
Project Manager:
Thomas Köhler
Exhibition Design:
Staples & Charles Ltd
Graphic Design:
Mary Mellerowicz Wolff
Consulting Typographer:
Julian Waters
Three-Dimensional Design:
Robert Staples
Project Size:
3,000 square feet
Project Budget:
$500,000

The Landeszeughaus, with more than 32,000 weapons and armors from the 15th to 17th centuries, is the largest extant arsenal from this period of European turbulence with almost continual sieges and battles between the Ottoman and Habsburg armies. As the Landeszeughaus is a central tourist attraction in Graz and the first of the Joanneum's 11 museums to be renovated, it was felt that a new standard of bilingual German and English text should be established.

In the large main texts – silkscreened on glass – the graphic design recognizes that the majority of visitors are German-speaking and that German is inherently longer than English. The German texts, on the left in Sabon, are higher and larger than the English, in Syntax, on the right. The location, size and contrasting serif and sanserif typefaces clearly differentiate the two languages. Historic quotations in both German and English are in Sabon Italic, each positioned above the title in their respective languages. The relative typefaces carry over for both languages in smaller texts along the reader rails.

1
For the title at the entry of the exhibition, Waters' calligraphy was enlarged to nearly eight feet in breadth, cut from polished steel, and mounted on a rust-red wall – a typographical salute to the armors fashioned of steel within, the red of the Habsburg imperial flag, and the commingling of metal and blood on the battlefield.

2
The rolled steel walls, the curves of the vaulted hall, the fluid nature of the calligraphy, and the gently curved rails combine into an integrated experience.

3
Bilingual exhibits pose challenging typographic and design problems. These are solved in this exhibit by using a serif typeface for German text, a sanserif typeface for the English translation, and by placing one language text above the other.

WHEN IT'S GONE? ¶ I DON'T KNOW THE ANSWERS, OF COURSE, BUT I'M LOOKING FORWARD TO FINDING OUT. AND I'M HOPING I'LL FIND A WINDOW THAT I CAN PEEK INTO

4
For the headlines, Julian Waters, one of America's finest calligraphers and typographers, was commissioned to create a script that reflects the handwritten official documents of the 15th to 17th centuries, while avoiding a similarity to "Fraktur" the historismus typeface that will forever be connected with the rise of the Third Reich.

5
The exhibition introduces visitors to the fabulous collection of arms and armor, explaining both their symbolic and military significance.

5

CONTRIBUTORS

BARBARA FAHS CHARLES, together with Robert Staples, established Staples & Charles Ltd more than 25 years ago to undertake museum interpretive planning and exhibition design at the highest creative and intellectual level. Ever since, Staples & Charles has been a leader in the world of museum design, a field that has expanded exponentially and become an identifiable discipline. Staples & Charles works nationally and internationally, with clients ranging from the Smithsonian Institution, the Canadian Museum of Civilization, and Monticello, to The Coca-Cola Company and South African Breweries. Ms. Charles' first experience with exhibition typography was orchestrating the typesetting – in linotype, ludlow and handset – for *Photography and the City*, designed by the Office of Charles and Ray Eames.

J. TEVERE MACFADYEN is a writer and exhibit developer and a principal of Main Street Design, an interpretive exhibition planning and design firm located in Cambridge, Massachusetts. Tevere was born in Rome, Italy and grew up in New York City, where the concept of interactivity takes on an entirely new meaning.

JANICE MAJEWSKI is the Smithsonian Institution's Accessibility Coordinator. Directing the Institution's Accessibility Program, she is responsible for coordinating the efforts of all of the museums, the National Zoo, and the Smithsonian's research facilities to become more accessible to staff and visitors with disabilities. Ms. Majewski began work at the Smithsonian in 1978, as the Coordinator for Special Education in the Office of Elementary and Secondary Education. She launched the Accessibility Program in early 1991.

Ms. Majewski has lectured extensively on museum accessibility. She has written a training manual called *Part of Your General Public Is Disabled* and has published the Smithsonian Guidelines for Accessible Exhibition Design. She is currently working with professionals throughout the Institution to develop guidelines for creating accessible facilities, programs, publications, and audiovisual productions.

MARY MCLAUGHLIN teaches environmental graphic and exhibit design at Virginia Commonwealth University. Previously, she was a project designer with Joseph A. Wetzel Associates in Boston, where she worked on projects for the Aerospace Museum in Los Angeles, California, the Maritime Center and Aquarium in Norwalk, Connecticut, and the Central Park and Bronx Zoos. As a consultant, she undertakes a wide variety of sign and exhibit design programs, including the comprehensive sign program for the Boston Common and the Emerald Necklace, in collaboration with her husband Tom McLaughlin. She has also collaborated with Zalisk Martin Associates in Cambridge, Massachusetts, on projects for the St. Louis Science Center, Dallas Science Center and the C.R. Smith Aviation Museum in Fort Worth, Texas.

DAVID STEADMAN is a founder of Observatory, an interdisciplinary collective of artists and designers. Residing in San Francisco, his activities range from graphic design consultation to video art.

DESIGN FIRMS AND ADDRESSES

The Burdick Group / 35 South Park Street / San Francisco, CA 94107 – 1806 / US
Christopher Chadbourne & Associates / 131 Mt. Auburn Street / Cambridge, MA 02138 / US
Drenttel Doyle Partners, Inc. / 1123 Broadway #600 / New York, NY 10010 / US
April Greiman / Greimanski Labs / 620 Moulton Avenue #211 / Los Angeles, CA 90031 / US
Victor Levie and Monique Rietbroek / Linnaeusparkweg 45 / 1098 Amsterdam / The Netherlands
Main Street Design / 875 Main Street / Cambridge, MA 02139 / US
Marit van der Meer and Josephine Oudijn / Linnaeusparkweg 45 / 1098 / Amsterdam / The Netherlands
Pentagram / 212 Fifth Avenue / New York, NY 10010 / US
Coco Raynes Associates, Inc. / 569 Boylston Street / Boston, MA 02116 / US
Jack Rouse Associates / 1014 Vine Street, Suite 1300 / Cincinnati, OH 45202 / US
Staples and Charles Ltd / 225 North Fairfax Street / Alexandria, VA 22314 – 2646 / US
Sussman/Prejza & Company, Inc. / 8520 Warner Drive / Culver City, CA 90232 / US
Trickett & Webb Limited / The Factory 84 Marchmont Street / London WC1N 1AG / UK
West Office Exhibition Design / 225 Third Street / Oakland, CA 94607 / US
Zalisk Martin Associates / 23 Arrow Street / Cambridge, MA 02138 / US

BIBLIOGRAPHY

Bringhurst, Robert. *The Elements of Typographic Style.* Second Edition. Washington: Hartley and Marks, 1997.

Carter, Rob, Ben Day, and Philip Meggs. *Typographic Design: Form and Communication.* Second Edition. New York: Van Nostrand Reinhold, 1993.

Finke, Gail Diebler. *You Are Here: Graphics That Direct, Explain & Entertain.* Cincinnati: St. Publications, Inc., 1999.

Graubard, Stephen, R. ed. *America's Museums.* Daedalus. Volume 128, Number 3 of the Proceedings of the American Academy of Arts and Sciences. Cambridge: Summer 1999.

Neuhart, John, Marilyn Neuhart, and Ray Eames. *Eames Design: The Work of the Office of Charles and Ray Eames.* New York: Harry N. Abrams, Incorporated, 1994.

Pazzuth, Krisztina. *Moholy – Nagy.* New York: Thames and Hudson Incorporated, 1985.

Society for Environmental Graphic Design. *The Americans with Disabilities Act White Paper.* Second Edition. Washington: 1993.

Spiekermann, Eric and E.M. Ginger. *Stop Stealing Sheep & Find Out How Type Works.* Mountain View: Adobe Press, 1993.

Staniszewski, Mary Anne. *The Power of Display: A History of Exhibition Installations at the Museum of Modern Art.* Cambridge: MIT Press, 1998.

Tupitsyn, Margarita with contributions by Matthew Drutt and Ulrich Pohlmann. *El Lissitzky: Beyond the Abstract Cabinet: Photography, Design, Collaboration.* New Haven: Yale University Press, 1999.

160

ACKNOWLEDGEMENTS

The authors wish to express thanks and gratitude to the many individuals who have made this book possible. The essays of Barbara Fahs Charles, Janice Majewski, Mary McLaughlin, and J. Tevere MacFadyen are not only informative; they reveal the passion and personal commitment required of anyone working in the field of exhibition design. We are deeply grateful for their words. Behind the scenes are many individuals associated with the exhibition design firms whose work is presented throughout the book. We thank them for taking time from their busy schedules to prepare visual examples, information, and written statements. We are indebted to David Steadman whose images, which appear on the cover and throughout the book's interior, express the potential of three-dimensional space in the realm of exhibition design. At Virginia Commonwealth University, Richard Toscan offered continuous support and encouragement. Our colleagues John Malinoski and Philip Meggs provided essential spiritual guidance. At RotoVision, we wish to thank Brian Morris for believing in this project and making it possible; and our copy editor, Kate Noël-Paton who prodded us along and brought precision and refinement to the text. Jerry Bates and his staff at the Graphics Lab provided exceptional production support for which we are most grateful. We wish to thank our families who endured the madness of the book's preparation and offered unending encouragement. A special thanks to Jamie, Syd, Jimmy, Muff, Linda, and Mark and for bringing smiles and helping us to keep things in perspective.